Lies o

Indispensabie Nation

D1284513

Lies of an
Indispensable Nation

Poems About the American Invasions of Iraq and Afghanistan

Lilvia Soto
Philadelphia, 8 February 2023

Lilvia Soto

atmosphere poress

© 2022 Lilvia Soto

Published by Atmosphere Press

Cover design by Josep Lledo

Muito obrigada, Ronaldo Alves.

Cover photo by Steve McCurry / Magnum Photos. Afghanistan. Helmand Province. 1980. A Father and son sit together.

No part of this book may be reproduced without permission from the author except in brief quotations and in reviews.

atmospherepress.com

With profound appreciation
this book is dedicated to

the friends who have inspired and encouraged me throughout the process of its writing, especially Michael Annis, Van K. Brock, Flavia M. Lobo, Yolanda Maltezos, Antonio Muñoz, Nora Nickerson, and Enrique Servín Herrera

David and Judy Ray, who taught me about the poetry of witness and protest

Pedro Lastra, who taught me to love poetry

my mother, Lilia Thayne, who was my first model of a just and compassionate human being

the police, firefighters, soldiers, and civilians who have suffered the violence of 9/11 and the Afghan and Iraq Wars, be they Afghans, Iraqis, Americans, members of the Coalition, journalists, or representatives of international organizations

every person who knows that an act of aggression against one is an injury to all and a diminishment of our shared humanity.

Contents

III. The Human Switch

IV. Waiting for the Barbarians

V. The Murdered

To ravage, to slaughter, to usurp under false titles,
they call empire, and where they make a desert, they call peace.

- Calgacus, Scots chieftain of the Caledonian Confederacy
Tacitus, *Dialogus Agricola Germania*

Introitus

Sometimes chance is kind to them, sometimes cruel.

But at the time their own destruction seems impossible to them. For they do not see that the force in their possession is only a limited quantity; nor do they see their relations with other human beings as a kind of balance between unequal amounts of force. Since other people do not impose on their movements that halt, that interval of hesitation, wherein lies all our considerations for our brothers in humanity, they conclude that destiny has given complete license to them, and none at all to their inferiors. And at this point they exceed the measure of the force that is actually at their disposal. Inevitably, they exceed it, since they are not aware that it is limited. And now we see them committed irretrievably to chance; suddenly things cease to obey them. Sometimes chance is kind to them, sometimes cruel.

- Simone Weil

Indispensable Nation

On 19 February 1998, Madeleine Albright, President Bill Clinton's Secretary of State, went on NBC's *The Today Show* to defend America's increasingly aggressive stance toward Iraq. "But if we have to use force, it is because we are America; we are the indispensable nation. We stand tall and we see further than other countries into the future, and we see the danger here to all of us." "Indispensable nation" was a phrase suggested to Albright by Sidney Blumenthal, who claims he coined it with historian James Chase "to describe the concept of the United States as the guarantor of stability as the sole superpower within the framework of multinational institutions." The phrase became a political cliché.

On 31 August 2016, former Secretary of State Hillary Clinton told the American Legion that the United States has "a unique and unparalleled ability to be a force for peace and progress, a champion for freedom and opportunity," and is therefore not just "an exceptional nation" but "the indispensable nation."

On 4 November 2016, President Barack Obama told HBO's Bill Maher, "We are *the* indispensable nation. People all over the world look to us, and follow our lead." "We really are the indispensable nation.... America is not just a great nation in the sense that it's powerful, but that our values and ideals actually matter."

On 18 January 2017, Vice President Joe Biden told the World Economic Forum, "And it is my hope and expectation that the next President and Vice President, and our leaders in Congress, will ensure that the United States continues to fulfill our historic responsibility as the indispensable nation."

But that's not all America has to be

"The disconnect between last Tuesday's monstrous dose of reality and the self-righteous drivel and outright deceptions being peddled by public figures and TV commentators is startling, depressing. The voices licensed to follow the event seem to have joined together in a campaign to infantilize the public. Where is the acknowledgment that this was not a 'cowardly' attack on 'civilization' or 'liberty' or 'humanity' or 'the free world' but an attack on the world's self-proclaimed superpower, undertaken as a consequence of specific American alliances and actions? How many citizens are aware of the ongoing American bombing of Iraq? And if the word 'cowardly' is to be used, it might be more aptly applied to those who kill from beyond the range of retaliation, high in the sky, than to those willing to die themselves in order to kill others. In the matter of courage (a morally neutral virtue): whatever may be said of the perpetrators of Tuesday's slaughter, they were not cowards.

"Our leaders are bent on convincing us that everything is O.K. America is not afraid. Our spirit is unbroken, although this was a day that will live in infamy and America is now at war. But everything is not O.K. And this was not Pearl Harbor. We have a robotic President who assures us that America still stands tall. A wide spectrum of public figures, in and out of office, who are strongly opposed to the policies being pursued abroad by this Administration apparently feel free to say nothing more than that they stand united behind President Bush. A lot of thinking needs to be done, and perhaps is being done in Washington and elsewhere, about the ineptitude of American intelligence and counter-intelligence, about options available to American foreign policy, particularly in the Middle East, and about what constitutes a smart program of military defense. But the public is not being asked to bear much of the burden of reality. The unanimously applauded, self-congratulatory bromides of a Soviet Party Congress seemed contemptible. The unanimity of the sanctimonious, reality-concealing rhetoric spouted by American officials and media commentators in recent days seems, well, unworthy of a mature democracy.

"Those in public office have let us know that they consider their task to be a manipulative one: confidence-building and grief management. Politics, the politics of a democracy—which entails disagreement, which promotes candor—has been replaced by psychotherapy. Let's by all means grieve together. But let's not be stupid together. A few shreds of historical awareness might help us understand what has just happened, and what may continue to happen. 'Our country is strong,' we are told again and again. I for one don't find this entirely consoling. Who doubts that America is strong? But that's not all America has to be."

—Susan Sontag, *The New Yorker*, 16 September 2001

No refuge from fate

The American military left Afghanistan a few hours before the 1 September deadline the Taliban had promised to enforce. Eleven days later, President Biden, former presidents Bill Clinton and Barack Obama and their wives commemorated, at Ground Zero, the 20th anniversary of the 9/11 attacks that served as an excuse for invading, first, Afghanistan, and a few months later, Iraq. Twenty years. The American occupation of Afghanistan lasted twenty years. That should have been enough time for the United States to be able to brag about having its own immortal epic poem. Twenty years should have been long enough not only to provide enough material worthy of the *Iliad,* but also of the *Odyssey.* After the end of the 10-year Trojan War, Odysseus, distinguished warrior and indispensable counsellor to the Greek enterprise, had enough time to visit the Land of the Lotus Eaters, to blind the Cyclops Polyphemus, to journey into Hades to consult the prophet Tiresias, to fight with the sea monster Scylla, to break away from the enticing arms of Circe and Calypso, to escape the lure of the sirens' song, and to finally return to his beloved kingdom in Ithaca and rescue his faithful Penelope from her greedy suitors.

Yes, the "longest" war was long enough, but it will not produce a single great epic, for America does not possess the Greek genius. Intoxicated with its possession of force, it glorifies its use in war and in politics and is willing to use it to turn men into things, as in slavery, the abuses of white supremacy, and the exploitation of workers at home and abroad. It is even willing to turn them into corpses, as in war, regime change, and colonization. America seems to be unaware that her force is limited and that her abuse of it will have serious consequences, for it is on loan from fate, and in the next turn of the wheel, it will be on loan to someone else, someone who will use it against her. This alternating retribution, according to Simone Weil, operates automatically to punish the abuse of force or power and is the main subject of Greek thought and the soul of the epic.

America has suffered this retribution, as in its loss of the Vietnam War, and now, its loss of the war on terror. It has suffered, but it has not learned. It has not learned about retribution to punish the abuse of power because it has not learned the meaning of limit, measure, and equilibrium as guides to a virtuous life. The Greeks knew, and they had, according to Weil, "the spiritual force that allowed them to avoid self-deception," and "to achieve in all their acts the greatest lucidity, purity, and simplicity" (Weil, 35).

America has not learned because it does not have the spiritual force to avoid self-deception, and because it would rather imitate the arrogance of the Romans and the Hebrews. The Romans considered themselves the nation destined to conquer and lead the world, and for two centuries, from 27 B.C., when Augustus Caesar became the first Roman emperor, to the death of Marcus Aurelius in 180 A.D., it did just that during its *Pax Romana*. During this period, the empire doubled its size, and it stretched from England to Egypt. It surrounded the Mediterranean Sea, and it included a quarter of the world's population. The George W. Bush administration was staffed with men who wrote and spoke frankly about their pursuit of a *Pax Americana* that would compare favorably with the *Pax Romana* they were trying to emulate.

Their program was based on three documents that built on each other over a period of 10 years and culminated on the September 2002 *The National Security Strategy of the United States*, known as the Bush Doctrine, a document that outlined President George W. Bush's national security policy, and according to which the United States reserved the option to wage a preventive war and opened the possibility for American use of nuclear weapons against nonnuclear states. At the time, it was claimed that the document had come out of the need to respond to the threats of international terrorism posed by the attacks of 11 September. The truth is that it came out of a previous plan for the creation of a global *Pax Americana*, written in September 2000 by the neo-conservative think tank Project for the New American Century (PNAC), and uncovered by the Scottish paper the *Sunday Herald*, that had been drawn for Dick Cheney, Donald Rumsfeld, Paul Wolfowitz, Jeb Bush, and Lewis Libby. This PNAC document, entitled *Rebuilding America's Defences: Strategies, Forces and Resources for A New Century,* revealed that even before he took office in January 2001, President Bush and his cabinet were planning a premeditated attack on Iraq to carry out regime change, and it is, like the document that preceded it and the one that followed it, a blueprint for maintaining global preeminence, precluding the rise of a great power rival, and shaping the international security order in line with American principles and interests for as far into the future as possible. This document was in turn built upon *The Defense Policy Guidance* (DPG), a strategy document drafted by the Cheney Defense Department in early 1992, during the administration of George Herbert Walker Bush, President George Walker Bush's father. The 3 documents shared the same godfathers and the same imperial goals and principles.

The *Pax Romana* or Roman Peace the Bush administration was trying to emulate was a 200-year period of peace within the Roman Empire, but as Edward Gibbon says, "They preserved peace by a constant preparation for war; and while justice regulated their conduct, they announced to the nations on their confines that they were as little disposed to endure as to offer an injury."[1] The Bush Agenda advocates dreamed, planned, and worked to create an all-powerful American Empire, sustained by the strongest and best prepared military money could buy, one they thought would be the best guarantor of peace in the world they were trying to subjugate for pride and profit. They wanted to use the military to americanize the world by exporting freedom, and by freedom they meant free trade or freedom of the corporations that would invade other countries, extract their natural resources, and exploit their peoples. According to their economic model, by removing restrictions, multinationals would be free to become engines of economic growth around the world. In reality, corporate globalization has created enormous wealth for Bechtel, Chevron, Lockheed Martin, Halliburton, Walmart, hundreds of other American corporations, their executives, stockholders, lobbyists, and friends in Congress, and dislocation, migration, abject poverty, suicide, and violence for the vast majority of the world's populations.

Of course, George Walker Bush and his followers were not the first Americans to promote the wealth of the elites with complete disregard for causing the poverty and misery of the masses. In the 20th Century, for example, between 1980 and 1990, President Ronald Reagan (with the help of British Prime Minister Margaret Thatcher), with his "Reaganomics" policies,

---

[1] Edward Gibbon, *The Decline and Fall of the Roman Empire*, abridged (New York: Dell, 1963), p. 33. Quoted in Antonia Juhasz, *The Bush Agenda: Invading the World, One Economy at a Time* Kindle Edition (Harper-Collins e-books, 2009), p. 25, Location 416.

which shifted the tax burden from the wealthy to the middle and lower income groups, poured vast sums of money into the military-industrial complex, gutted social welfare programs, and reduced labor protections, achieved a massive redistribution of income from the poor to the wealthy (Juhasz, 66-69).

In a larger historical context, for examples of Western colonialism's conquest and exploitation of humans and the environment, we can go back to 1602 when the Dutch East India Company was established as the world's first major corporation and, a few years later, in 1621, unable to enforce a trade monopoly on their nutmeg and mace, emptied the Banda Islands in the Maluccas, or Spice Islands, by burning their buildings to the ground and torturing and butchering their inhabitants, or sending them as slaves to Java or Sri Lanka. As the Bush cabal did four centuries later in Iraq, the Dutch thought that once the Bandanese were gone, settlers and slaves could be brought in to create a new economy in the archipelago (Ghosh, 5-30). Or perhaps we can go back to 1545 when Spain opened the world's largest silver mine in Potosí, Bolivia, making the Spanish Empire one of the richest in the world, where thousands of indigenous people and African slaves died through accidents, brutal treatment, or poisoning by the mercury used in the extraction process. Or we can go further back to the 1494 Treaty of Tordesillas, which divided the world beyond Europe between Spain to the west and Portugal to the east of an imaginary line drawn down the middle of the Atlantic, a treaty which was the result of *Inter caetera*, the 1493 papal bull of Alexander VI, born Rodrigo de Borja in Valencia, Spain, whereby he devided the undiscovered world between the two Iberian countries. Or we can even go back to 1455, when Pope Nicholas V in his *Romanus pontifex* bull granted the Portuguese a perpetual monopoly in trade with Africa and allowed the permanent enslavement of any and all people they encountered south of Cape Bojador, on the coast of western Sahara (McCoy and Wikipedia).

If we limit ourselves to the United States, the difference be-tween the policies of previous American presidents and George W. Bush's, according to Antonia Juhasz, is that the Bush Doctrine, which was based on the international finance system forged in 1944 at the Bretton Woods, New Hampshire, conference, which created the International Monetary Fund and the World Bank, also had the additional help of the 1995 formation of the World Trade Organization. While the WTO pushed financial deregulation, protected Big Pharma's medical patents, and removed restrictions on genetically modified food crops, the IMF and the World Bank pressed "structural adjustment programs" on developing economies. As Alfred McCoy says, "With this powerful one-two punch, neoliberal economists smashed tariff barriers worldwide, helping create a unified capitalist market that covered the globe" (McCoy, 331-332).

The Bush Doctrine made economics a weapon of war. The United States military invasion of Iraq assured that not only was the head of their government replaced (assassinated), but also that by having the U.S. write their new constitution, their existing laws on trade, public services, banking, taxes, agriculture, investment, foreign ownership, media, and oil, among others, would also be replaced by new laws favorable to American corporations (Juhasz, 7-8).

In a letter submitted to the United Nations Security Council on 8 May 2003, the United States, on behalf of the Coalition Provisional Authority, promised to "exercise powers of government, temporarily, and as necessary," and to provide "for the responsible administration of the Iraqi financial sector, for humanitarian relief, for economic reconstruction, for the transparent operation and repair of Iraq's infrastructure and natural resources, and for the progressive transfer of administrative responsibilities to such representative institutions of government." With this letter, the Bush administration secured the passage of UN Security Council Resolution 1438, by which the Security Council acknowledged the occupation of Iraq by the Coalition and recognized the Coalition Provisional Authority as the occupation government.

The Security Council added some specifications, such as the obligation of the CPA to promote the welfare of the Iraqi people by restoring security and stability and by ensuring that the Iraqi people can "freely determine their own political future." The Security Council also asked the CPA to comply with their international obligations as specified in the Geneva Conventions of 1949 and the Hague Regulations of 1907 (Juhasz, 187-188).

> Article 43 of the Hague Regulations (ratified by the United States) requires that an occupying power "take all the measures in his power to restore, and ensure, as far as possible, public order and safety, while respecting, unless absolutely prevented, the laws in force in the country."

Provision #363 of the U.S. Army's Law of Land Warfare repeats Article 43 word for word. The legal interpretation of these and related provisions is that an occupier is required to ensure that the lights are on, the water is flowing, the streets are safe, and the basic necessities of life are provided. However, the occupier is not permitted to make changes beyond those necessary to meet these obligations (Juhasz, 188).

Not only did the Bush administration not obey its international obligations, or the promises it made to the Security Council, but instead it did the exact opposite. Under L. Paul Bremer III, the appointed administrator of the CPA, it wrote its new constitution and radically altered Iraq's laws in order to restructure its entire economy, from a state to a market economy that guarantees "free markets, free trade and private property," for its only aim was to open Iraq to American corporations. The result was that while the new laws freed multinationals from government regulations, the rest of society suffered enormous amounts of economic and social insecurity. And Iraq was only the first step. The plans were to expand this agenda to countries across the Middle East. The Bush administration did what most United States administrations have done throughout its history: lied to American citizens, to the United Nations, to the entire world, in pursuit of building and securing the American Empire.

There is one aspect of the *Pax Romana*, however, that the Bush team rejected: the commitment to public works. Augustus invested in water aqueducts so that they reached all the regions, including the poorest, of the city. He built roads, bridges, public housing, public baths, theaters, and temples. He invested in culture and the arts; many of the works that constitute what is called today the Western canon were written at that time. The Bush administration, in contrast, reduced federal spending on vital public needs, such as affordable public housing, health care, child care, programs to address hunger and poverty, as well as funding for universities and the arts. The Bush Doctrine supporters argued that only an unrivaled *Pax Americana* that included corporate globalization could guarantee world peace, and maintaining it justified unlimited defense spending, perpetual war, and the complete disregard of freedom, democracy, and the needs of its citizens (Juhasz, 24-27).

Twenty years after *The National Security Strategy*, the three-stage (1992-2000-2002) document that served as the basis for invading Iraq and Afghanistan, and after suffering an ignominious defeat in both places, the US., even though it still has the world's largest armed forces, has finally abandoned the ambition of having a military capable of fighting two wars at the same time. Although it has generally, though reluctantly, been accepted that the United States' unipolar moment has passed, the AUKUS deal with Britain to build nuclear submarines for Australia demonstrates that the United States is trying to contain China, the country it sees as the principal challenger to its global primacy. However, most world affairs specialists agree that the period we are entering is going to be multipolar rather than bipolar, with China, Russia, India, Europe and other centers, including non-state actors, gaining power relative to America.

On 10 September 2013, President Barack Obama in his remarks to the nation on Syria said that America is not the world's policeman. Clearly, that should not prevent the United States from becoming the leading problem solver of the new multipolar world, or as Richard N. Haass, president of the Council on Foreign Relations, said in his 2019 essay "How a World Order Ends," "resurrecting the old order will be impossible," but, he added, "The United States must show restraint and recapture a degree of respect in order to regain its reputation as a benign actor" and save the world from "deeper disarray" or even "trends that spell catastrophe."

In the remarks he delivered before the 76th Session of the United Nations General Assembly on 21 September 2021, President Biden said:

Simply put: We stand, in my view, at an inflection point in history. And I'm here today to share with you how the United States intends to work with partners and allies to answer these questions and the commitment of my new administration to help lead the world toward a more peaceful, prosperous future for all people.

Instead of continuing to fight the wars of the past, we are fixing our eyes on devoting our resources to the challenges that hold the keys to our collective future: ending this pandemic; addressing the climate crisis; managing the shifts in global power dynamics; shaping the rules of the world on vital issues like trade, cyber, and emerging technologies; and facing the threat of terrorism as it stands today.

In the same speech, he said: "I stand here today, for the first time in 20 years, with the United States not at war. We've turned the page." His proud declaration came only three weeks after an American drone killed a family of 10 civilians in the last act of our 20-year occupation of Afghanistan, a tragic mistake that was first called "righteous" by General Mark A. Milley, Chairman of the Joint Chiefs of Staff. The day before his declaration, the United States had launched an air strike in Syria, and 3 weeks earlier, one in Somalia. Biden seems to have forgotten that the American military is still fighting in Iraq, Yemen, Syria, Libya, Somalia, and Niger (Marjorie Cohn).

In his first foreign policy address, he said: "We are ending all American support for offensive operations in the war in Yemen, including relevant arms sales" (Petersen-Smith). Did he forget? The U.S. is selling Saudi Arabia $650 million worth of missiles and providing $500 million worth of maintenance for U.S.-made aircraft, training, and other support for its military operations. The U.S. is doing this at the moment when Saudi Arabia is escalating its bombing in Yemen. I am sure he has not forgotten that he promised to continue launching "over-the-horizon" attacks in Afghanistan, where we no longer have boots on the ground. The day before he made this announcement, on 20 September, Dave Philipps of the *New York Times* revealed that on the 12th of that month, approximately 2000 soldiers of the First Stryker Brigade Combat Team, Fourth Infantry Division, had deployed to Iraq from Fort Carson, Colorado, for a nine-month combat tour "in harm's way" (Philipps). This was just before President Biden and Iraqi Prime Minister Mustafa al-Kadhimi met at the White House on 26 July and announced a shift in the U.S. military mission to a purely advisory role by the end of the year (White House, "Readout"). Was Dave Philipps wrong about the soldiers of the First Stryker Brigade Combat Team being in harm's way when they got to Iraq? Was he unaware of the deal Iraqi Prime Minister al-Kadhimi and President Biden were going to make on 26 July? Did he say that because until the end of the year they will still be on a military mission? Or is the reality that even in an advisory capacity, soldiers are always in harm's way?

President Biden also promised, "And as the United States seeks to rally the world to action, we will lead not just with the example of our power but, God willing, with the power of our example." Sadly, although he said "Our approach is firmly

16

grounded and fully consistent with the United Nations' mission and the values we have agreed to when we drafted this Charter. These are commitments we all made and that we are all bound to uphold," and swore "adherence to international laws and treaties," his drone strikes of the past and those he promises with his "over-the-horizon" policy, as well as those of his predecessors, violate both the United Nations Charter and the Geneva Conventions. His administration is also violating international law by maintaining the use of Title 42 to deny migrants, including asylum seekers, access at the U.S.-Mexico border. He has also reopened detention centers used by the Trump administration, and the number of detainees at these places have grown to 22,000, a 56 percent increase since the day he took office.

As Andrew J. Bacevich and Annelle Sheline have so eloquently pointed out, if Biden is sincere about what he said at the U.N., he needs to do several things:

The first is to explicitly revoke the Bush Doctrine, unambiguously reinstating self-defense as the dominant rationale for the use of U.S. military force. Maintaining a position of global primacy has always been the implicit, made explicit in the Bush Doctrine, objective of the foreign policy establishment of the United States, whose members take it for granted that the United States should enjoy certain prerogatives and be exempt from obeying rules and treaties it does not like. If he is sincere, he should make it clear that the United States will play by the same rules governing the use of force that it expects other countries to play by. If he wants to lead by example, he should bring the United States into compliance with preexisting norms. As Noam Chomsky said, "Once we abstract ourselves from thinking 'we are exceptional' and universalise issues, we start treating ourselves by the same standards that we apply to others. Why treat ourselves differently? Once we face this question, the world looks very different" ("on the cruelty of American imperialism").

President Biden should close the detention facility in Guantánamo Bay, Cuba, and affirm the renewed U.S. compliance with the Convention Against Torture. He should also convince the Senate to ratify several key treaties and international agreements, including the UN Convention on the Law of the Sea (1982), the Comprehensive Nuclear Test Ban Treaty (1996), the Mine Ban Treaty, or Ottawa Treaty (1997), and the Rome Statute of the International Criminal Court (1998).

The Fourth Geneva Convention defines collective punishment as a war crime. By that standard, U.S. economic sanctions targeting Cuba, Venezuela, and others are illegal and immoral.

As a signatory to the Nuclear Nonproliferation Treaty (NPT), the United States has promised to "pursue negotiations in good faith" leading to "nuclear disarmament." If the president means to lead by example, he should consider refurbishing rather than replacing the U.S. nuclear arsenal. He should also promise to forego the option of a nuclear first strike and pledge "no-first-use."

If he is sincere about wanting to lead the world "toward a more peaceful, prosperous future for all people," he needs to be aware that "national security" no longer means addressing military threats only, that many of the threats to the safety and well-being of American citizens come from the weather, pandemics, poverty, racism, the gun culture, inequity in access to voting rights, educational, medical, and social safety net resources, and a deeply divided society, half of it willing to resort to insurrections to deprive the other half of its rights. If he is serious about wanting to improve the lives of Americans, he needs to be willing to admit that there is an imbalance in the resources allocated to the Pentagon ($778 billion in new military spending for 2022) and the agencies in charge of dealing with national problems, such as the Coast Guard, the National Institutes of Health, the U.S. Forest Service, and the U.S. Border Patrol.

If he really wants to work towards a more peaceful world for all people, he should begin to trim the Empire's footprint by reducing the number of overseas bases. Currently there are some 750 in over 80 countries. He should also close one or more of the six regional combatant commands that oversee military operations across vast geographic areas of the earth. He should also curb the export of U.S. manufactured weapons, which in 2020 amounted to $175 billion. It is simply not possible to be for peace if manufacturing the weapons designed to kill millions of your fellow human beings is one of your main industries.

The George Walker Bush adepts made it clear that they were working to create a *Pax Americana* that would imitate and surpass the *Pax Romana* of 2000 years ago. As Joseph Nye says: "Rome succumbed not to the rise of a new empire, but to internal decay and a death of a thousand cuts from various barbarian groups." Although the United States is facing in China the economic and military competition of a new empire for global hegemony, the American Empire is more likely to succumb first to countless forms of internal decay and to the myriad cuts inflicted by the barbarians living inside its own borders. As Francis Fukuyama says: "The hallmark of a mature democracy is the ability to carry out peaceful transfers of power following elections, a test the country failed spectacularly on January 6th."

In "The Iliad, or the Poem of Force," Mary McCarthy's English translation of "L'Iliade, ou le poème de la force," first published in the November 1945 issue of *Politics,* philosopher Simone Weil ends her essay by saying:

> In spite of the brief intoxication induced at the time of the Renaissance by the discovery of Greek literature, there has been, during the course of twenty centuries, no revival of the Greek genius. Something of it was seen in Villon, in Shakespeare, Cervantes, Molière, and--just once--in Racine. The bones of human suffering are exposed in *L'école de femmes* and in *Phèdre*, love being the context--a strange century indeed, which took the opposite view from that of the epic period, and would only acknowledge human suffering in the context of love, while it insisted on swathing with glory the effects of force in war and in politics. To the list of writers given above, a few other names might be added. But nothing the peoples of Europe have produced is worth the first known poem that appeared among them. Perhaps they will yet rediscover the epic genius, when they learn that there is no refuge from fate, learn not to admire force, not to hate the enemy, not to scorn the unfortunate. How soon this will happen is another question.

Sequence

Nero

And what's going on in Nero's mind as he watches Iraq burn?
Does it please him that he awakens a memory in the history of the
jungle that preserves his name as an enemy of Hamurabbi and
Gilgamesh and Abu Nuwas: My law is the mother of all laws, the
flower of eternity grows in my fields, and poetry – what does that
mean?

(....)

And what goes on in Nero's mind as he watches the world burn? I
am master of the Day of Judgement. Then he orders the camera to
stop rolling, because he doesn't want anyone to see that his fingers
are on fire at the end of this long American movie!

—Mahmoud Darwish, *A River Dies of Thirst*

The Rite of Night

In medieval towns all over Spain,
cigüeñas build church belfry nests,
while from Madrid,
the Falange heir
flies to join his triplets
from across the seas,
to scream with them
¡Viva la muerte!
Long live death!

—"The Rite of Night"

A Birthday, Almost

11 September 2002

When will our consciences grow so tender that we will act to prevent human misery rather than avenge it?

—Eleanor Roosevelt

Today should have been my birthday.

A year ago, for the first time,
watching the towers crumble, the fires ignite,
the bodies fall, the steel twist,
the bodies fall,
I felt American.

As time passed, the bodies were buried,
heroes honored,
mothers and husbands mourned.
Ground Zero was cleared,
the Pentagon rebuilt,
the dust removed.

Today should have been my birthday.

It would have been a glorious celebration
with American flags fluttering
in schools, embassies, and mountain tops,
with my heart aching in unison
with the hearts of people
from every town and village
on every continent and island.

I saw rose petals floating down
from Saint Paul's dome in London,
listened to the chanted prayers
of Buddhist monks in Tokyo,
heard the strains of Mozart's *Requiem*
played in every church and concert hall
in every time zone around the earth.

I was stirred with the towers of light
that illuminated the skies of Paris,
and I grieved for the dead
with my brothers and sisters
from every barrio and every hamlet
around the earth.

Today should have been my birthday.

But before the first Buddhist chant,
the first *Requiem* note,
the first petal of a rose,
we heard the beating of the drums:

Depose Sadam, the evil one.
We are the Super Power,
they will be with us,
or against us,
those men and women
from around the earth.

Today should have been my birthday.

Mothers' Hearts

11 September 2002

They disappeared,
dust vilified,
in a foreign land.

The fire they ignited
feeds
the acrid smells of memory.

Church bells toll around the earth,
but not for them.
We pray, light candles, hold vigils,
but not for them.

Their mothers carried them in joy,
delivered them in pain,
suckled them in love.

Their mothers' hearts have a hole
seven-stories deep,
but cannot pray on worshipped soil.

Flames burn, roses grow,
on earth made sacred by mothers' tears.
White doves fly, voices ring
in air hallowed by mothers' grief.

Rose Valiant[2]

For Michael Edward Roberts

With moisture in his eyes,
sorrow in his fingertips,
his father caresses the replica of shield 6611,
the one Michael wore on September 11[th,]
the one he wore before Michael,
when he was a New York City firefighter.

His little sister Karen
listens for the voice she'll never hear again,
and redoubles her efforts in school,
to honor her brother's memory.

His mother tends to the Irish roses
he wanted her to plant.
Her garden has nine sides by eleven panels high.
His special blossoms are the first sign of dawn
she sees every morning.

Her eyes moisten their petals,
her fingertips, their thorns.
Her husband reminds her,
Ronnnie, it is what it is.
She has it written on a piece of oak tag paper.

More numerous than the orange petals
are her incantations,
It is what it is.

---

[2] This family's story appeared in *The New York Times,* 11 Sept. 2006.
Web.

Blue Man[3]

The anthropologists call him Blue Man
because of his ink blue shirt
and his blue-striped pants,
because as he lies tangled in a mass grave
his arms tied with rope,
his skull jerked upward at the neck,
his sand-colored cap firm on his skull,
his eyes blindfolded with frayed cloth,
his mouth open wide with pain,

the crack of the bullet hovers,
the shimmer of the blueflies blinds,
the scent of the starry Prussian scilla rises,
and the sorrow of the flute cut from its reedbed
whispers
through threadbare clouds
to the azure sky.

They call him Blue Man
because of his presence,
blue like the fragile veins
in the stilled eye of the turtledove.

They call him Blue Man
because of the longing for being
that echoes
in the heart of the despot.

---

[3] Inspired by Burns, John F. "Uncovering Iraq's Horrors in Desert
Graves." *The New York Times*, 5 June 2006. Web.

The Kiss

Halabja made the twins of Hiroshima and Nagasaki into triplets.
—Hashim Kochani, *Halabja*

Black clouds smelling of garlic and sweet apple
fill the morning sky,
within minutes,
the tender spring leaves begin falling off the fig trees,
and the partridge in the cage falls on its back.

When he looks out,
Abdullah sees the sheep and the goats
dead in the yard,
and lying by his neighbors' well,
little Bereavan, her pigtails undone,
her green eyes shut.

He walks to the village,
where a sheet of red and white butterflies
covers the Sirwan,
and the bodies of his neighbors, its banks.

Turning a body over,
he gasps,
it's his mother.
Holding her in his arms,
he wants to kiss her forehead,
her cheeks, her hand,
her hair, at least her hair,
just one tender kiss.
His heart says *Yes,*
his mind says *No,*
he can die from the chemicals
that killed her.

Still today,
Abdullah grieves for the kiss.

In Paupers' Field: The Tiffany Angel[4]

The large refrigerator in the morgue
at Basra Maternity
holds thirteen tiny bodies.
Wrapped in bedsheets,
they lie in cardboard boxes
used to ship packets of cereal.

Some days there is electricity,
some days there isn't,
it is the midsummer season,
and the stench of decaying angels fills the air.

This is the refrigerator
where they keep the infants
whose parents cannot pay
three dollars for a burial.
They will keep them for a week,
then bury them in Paupers' Field.

A new box arrives marked
Tiffany Milk Biscuits,
without biscuits,
filled with a new angel.
Cause of death?

Sanctions, says the doctor.

---

[4] Based on Brown, Matthew Hay. "Iraqi Sanctions: Without Medicine and Supplies, The Children Die." *CommonDreams.org News Center.* Published in *The Hartford Courant, 23* Oct. 2000. Web.

Curious Shapes[5]

But the hearts of small children are delicate organs. A cruel beginning
in this world can twist them into curious shapes.

—Carson McCullers

The bombing destroyed its electrical system,
shut down its water purification plants.
Thousands died of cholera,
thousands died of typhoid fever,
infants died, thousands and thousands died.

Thirteen years later,
one of every three Iraqi children was stunted,
thousands malnourished,
wasting,
stunted.

The Pentagon admitted it wanted to accelerate
the effects of the sanctions,
leave behind pools of soaring bacteria counts,
a killer that would keep killing.

An Air Force planner said,
We will not tolerate Sadam,
get rid of the guy
and we'll fix your electricity.

But the hearts of the empire's children
are delicate organs,
when they grow up
wrapped in cruelty towards others,
they can twist in curious ways
and grow up as model engines
of the empire of stunted souls.

---

[5] Inspired by Bovard, James. "Iraqi Sanctions and American Intentions:
Blameless Carnage? Part I." *The Future of Freedom Foundation.*
Originally published in the Jan. 2004 edition of *Freedom Daily.*

Preemption

If left unchecked, Iraq would most likely have a nuclear weapon in
this decade. The president of the United States could not afford to
trust Saddam's motives or give him the benefit of the doubt.
—Condoleeza Rice, National Security Adviser

If left unchecked,
you and I could
in this or the next decade
commit a crime.
The president should not take a chance.

If left unchecked,
the fetus in every pregnant woman's womb
could
in this century
become a terrorist.
The president should not take a chance.

Before War

15 March 2003

Seven women gather to share photos,
memories, words.

This calm Tucson day we invoke
the fragrance of alfalfa fields,
a favorite aunt's 1942 wedding,
debonair Grandpa's collection of hats,
the play of light and shadow
on waters that sway a beloved boat.

Lisa's heart aches for her friend
who is moving away
and for her friend's two-year-old grandson,
who will be left bereft of a grandmother's care.

This sunny day I listen to Leslie's
artful planting of words
in our minds' eyes,
as she will this afternoon
arrange in soil
the rose bushes she carries in her van.

Rita talks of her young German mother
standing in a scatter of stars,
curving her glimmering body
towards her immigrant dream.

This primavera day Dennie searches
for words for her sons,
as she touches the reflection of her dreams
in those other shores.

Anita remembers a Paris vacation
and dreams of other adventures.

Sarah of the inward look
and the prayerful voice
talks of words she needs
to describe her illness,
exorcise it,
perhaps.

This luminous day I hear her desire
to touch silence,
comfort others.

Seven women gather
around Rita's table,
our quiet understanding,
an eye of warmth and stillness
in the gathering storm.

This brilliant day I hear wings beating
as the fates from London,
Washington, and Madrid
fly to the Azores,
in their hands,
spindle and scissors.

The Rite of Night

15 March 2003

Around the Alcázar and Catedral
bridal azahar perfumes Seville.
The sun shines at night in golden skies,
black swallows dance
the birth of spring.

In medieval towns all over Spain,
cigüeñas build church belfry nests,
while from Madrid,
the Falange heir
flies to join his triplets
from across the seas,
to scream with them,
¡Viva la muerte!
Long live death!

The Swallows of Baghdad

19 March 2003

They're smart,
can pinpoint a single palace,
cut through iron, stone, and marble,
find Saddam and his sons
deep underneath.

Against the explosions,
I see a bird.
It surprises me more than the bombs.
I see two birds,
then hundreds cross
in front of the camera,
wheel around.

Six years ago
I spent every orange-blossomed April evening
watching the swallows of Seville
glide into air.

The swallows of Baghdad do not dance
the symphony of wind.
Their flight is jagged,
their turns desperate.

Is there a shriek
or a whimper
I do not hear
against the crumbling imperial marble
and the explosions?

Coda: Atocha -- 11 March 2004

Is their flight still jagged,
are their turns desperate?
Do they shriek in Baghdad?
Do they whimper in Madrid?

Will there be orange blossoms in Seville?
¿Volverán las oscuras golondrinas?[6]
Will they bring another spring?

---

[6] Bécquer, Gustavo Adolfo. "Volverán las oscuras golondrinas."

Immigrant Eyes

For Fernando Suárez del Solar

In peace the sons bury their fathers,
but in war the fathers bury their sons.

—Croesus

The first week, I turn on the news, see
thick bushy brows,
dark long lashes,
soulful Giancarlo Giannini eyes,
hear a soft Spanish voice say
he did not want his son to go to Iraq,
but the boy insisted.
They're recent immigrants from Tijuana,
the boy wanted to prove his patriotism.

Three days later, I turn on the news, see
thick bushy brows,
dark long lashes,
bottomless immigrant eyes,
hear an old Spanish voice say,

Oh, yes, they will send me a medal,
give me a flag,
but my life is ruined,
and my grandson will not know his father.

The Promise

28 March 2003

After John F. Burns

And they promised the soldiers
sweets and flowers and jubilant smiles
but forgot prayers for them to go home.

A bomb falls on the crowded marketplace of Shula,
kills and injures merchants and early-evening shoppers.
Six-year-old Iman Fadil dies,
her mother and little brother die too.

As they pick up her tiny body to wash it,
the faithful in the mosque break into chanting,
Lā 'ilāha 'ila Allāh,
Wa muhammad rasūl Allāh.
"There is no God but God,
and Muhammad is his messenger."

In the primeval darkness,
the imam prays
for the Muslims who have died,
for the ones who cling to life,
for the Americans and the British to go home,
leave the Iraqis in their Iraqi land.

In a casket big enough for a man,
through the flickering shadows
of the ancient city in mourning
Iman goes home
accompanied by the rhythmic *Shahādah,*
Lā 'ilāha 'ila Allāh,
Wa muhammad rasūl Allāh.

Afterimage

April 2003

A man sits on a dirt road,
left leg bent, touching right ankle,
right leg stretched out,
rifle by his side,
feet anchored,
shoulders stooped,
head bent under helmet.

Through heavy smoke,
people rush past.

A man sits on a dirt road,
arms heavy with
small body
they hold.

Album I

For José Couso

In Albukamal camp in Syria,
Nawal Dahdouh clasps seven-year-old Alahmad
to her breast,
says,

I left Baghdad because I don't want
my only son to die.
I have already lost two.

Blood runs down the lens.
The splattered camera lies unclaimed
on the floor of the Palestine Hotel.
A family mourns in Spain.

Loss of life is regrettable, says the President.
We do everything we can to minimize it,
we use smart bombs.

Soldiers. Journalists. Civilians.
We don't know their names,
their stories, their loves.
Hundreds of thousands.
It is regrettable.

Album II: Anfalisation

For Martin Sullivan, Chairman of the U.S. President's Advisory Committee on Cultural Property

A statue of Saddam Hussein was pulled down on Wednesday, in the most staged photo-opportunity since Iwo Jima.

—Robert Fisk

The statue of Saddam falls
falls
falls.
Our soldiers watch the statue of Saddam
fall
while collectors stash antiquities.

Mobs ransack the cradle of civilization
while our soldiers watch
or collect souvenirs.

Five thousand years of art lost
while our soldiers watch the statue of Saddam
fall.

In the midst of war,
looting is unfortunate,
says our Secretary of Defense.
Antiquities?
He knows everything begins tomorrow.
And his mission is destruction.

On top of his tank
Alex Rivera looks in the children's eyes,
sings with them.
In the midst of war,
singing is a miracle.

Five thousand years of historical memory
destroyed.
Halliburton did not get
a multi-billion dollar contract
to protect it.
It is unfortunate.

Carpe Diem

Gather ye rosebuds while ye may,
Old Time is still a-flying,
And this same flower that smiles today
Tomorrow will be dying.

—Robert Herrick (1591-1674)

Ted Koppel asks the soldier
if he knows the meaning
of the Latin expression
painted on the gun of his tank.
Seize the day is the soft answer.

The soldier and the anchorman expand
their discussion about the Horatian phrase,
but do not tell us
who must seize the day,
or for what.

Must our soldiers seize it
to fly more sorties,
drop more bombs,
kill more children?

Should they seize it for themselves?
Take a shower?
Dream of a long sleep
in a clean bed
without thunder, smoke, or danger?

And their targets?
The two-year-old girl
whose head was blown away
the second day?
The children who lie wounded
in a hospital without water,
medicine, or lights?
The two men who embrace

in the middle of the street
to cry for their wives and children
killed in the first day's bombardment?

They lived near the restaurant
where an intelligence agent said
Saddam would be holding a meeting.

Saddam escaped.
He seized the day.

Minimal

For Rubén Moreno Valenzuela

Analysts say the cost of overestimating the threat posed by Mr.
Hussein was minimal, while the cost of underestimating it could have
been incalculable.

$\qquad$ —*The New York Times*, 20 July 2003

At Queen Mary's Hospital
Ali Abbas is fitted with prosthetic arms.
Robin Cooper, a specialist in prosthetics,
says the boy

should be able to live a nearly normal life,
for with artificial limbs
people can drive cars--
even fly light aircraft.

Soon Ali will understand that all
he wants to do
is hold his beloved in his arms and
caress the sweet skin of his first-born.

Maybe then he will learn
to throw grenades
with his prosthetic hands.

Mamá bonita

For Kaden Dawson

The mere thought of what could have happened
kept you awake.
You would have gone insane
without his little arms around your neck,
without his sweet voice to say
Mamá bonita.

Did you see
the girl with head and feet in bloody bandages,
a vacant look in her eyes?
She was your daughter's age.
Her black-draped mother sat by her side.
It was the first week, they still had medicines.

The boy who lost both arms from the shoulders?
He also lost both parents
and all his brothers.
He looked about eleven,
like your first-born.

And the two-year-old whose head
was blown away the second day?
She was the age of your baby.
They carried her out in a rug.

After our victory,
a family of six was blown up
in an explosion of munitions
we did not guard.

Did you see the lone survivor--
the child with face bloodied,
body mangled?
He resembles your four-year-old,
your dark-haired boy of soulful eyes
who wraps his little arms around your neck
and whispers
Mamá bonita.

Muqawama:[7] The Lion and the Mosquito

نإ ةضوعبلا يمدُت ةلقُم َسلا

"A mosquito can make the lion's eye bleed"

I

Before the invasion,
the Bush administration declared,

He's a dictator pursuing
and possessing
weapons for the purpose of inflicting
death on a large scale.
Wars are not won on the defensive,
we must take the battle to the enemy.

And to the enemy they took their weapons,
the largest, most technologically advanced
manned and unmanned
legal and illegal
smart and not-so-smart
arsenal ever designed by man
or the devil
to destroy present and future life.

One of them was an ingenious,
fertile, cluster bomb
ready to give birth
to her little bomblets,
entrust them with carrying out their heritage,
their mission of spreading death
to children not yet born
or conceived,
to explode,
years from now,
on women in black,
veterans on crutches,
boys kicking ball,
lovers holding hands,
girls whispering.

---

[7] Arabic for "resistance."

II

A video reveals the war preparations
of the dangerous dictator.
A few days before the invasion,
elegant in his double-breasted gray suit,
Saddam aims a slingshot,
shoots an arrow,
swings a Molotov cocktail,
urges his generals
to mass produce this arsenal,
get it into the hands of his people.

The small weapons and explosives
they hide around the country
sustain *muqawama*.

III

He has destroyed the mosquito,
but the blood in his eye
obscures the victory
the lion thought was his.

Suqut

Many in Iraq called the war the *suqut.* "It remained open-ended, its muddled aftermath as inconclusive as Hussein's fall seemed climactic. For Iraqis, *suqut* meant an end without renewal, a seemingly endless interim. It was a life imposed, not chosen."

—Anthony Shadid, *The Eyes of Amal*

Tomorrow[8]

For Terry Michael Lisk

Only the dead have seen the end of war.
> —Plato

His bloodstained boot forgotten on the sand,
the soldier is taken
to the improvised morgue,
from where they carry him
to the helicopter
making its nightly rounds
on the desert landing strip.

Under the star-lit night,
six carry him,
sixty wait, heads bowed,
to salute the comrade going home.

They sense by tomorrow
one of them will have seen
the end of war.

---

[8] Inspired by the video *Good-bye to an American Soldier.* Narrated by Dexter Filkins. *The New York Times,* 29 June 2006, and by his accompanying article "The Iraqi War Ends in Silence for an American Soldier."

The Bodywasher

You must start at a young age in order to get accustomed to working
with the dead.
  —Raid Hashem, who began washing bodies when he was ten.

Humming the prayers recited
when a daughter loses her mother,
or a mother, her daughter,
Khalila washes the victim
of the mosque explosion.

Competent and compassionate,
the body washer prepares the young teacher,
or what remains of her.

With the mother's help,
she opens the blanket wrapped around the body,
and the broken string of prayer beads
rolls down at their feet.

They cut away the shredded abaya,
splash the body with camphor water,
sprinkle it with fragrant powdered soap,
scrub off the blood,
let the pink rivulet
run off into the gutter.

Khalila pads the wounds with cotton wads,
wraps the body in a shroud,
a plastic sheet,
a second shroud.

The mother sprays perfume
over her daughter,
remembers when she could hold
her tight little bundle,
sobs,

I was waiting
for you to wash me.
Look what happened.
Who will wash me now?

Let them wear mink

Semper Fidelis

To the brave men of Company Echo

They placed dummy marines made of
cardboard cutouts and camouflage shirts
in observation posts along desert highways.

They scrounged for armor,
swept roads for bombs,
held their Humvee doors shut
with their hands,

but the explosives were powerful,
the steel of the company's
scraps, too short.

With no devices
to block makeshift bombs,
the young men of Company E lost
limbs and lives in Ramadi.

Better for them to have made
a dummy president,
a dummy secretary of defense,
an entire dummy congress,
to place along the halls of power,
and take the flesh ones to Ramadi.

Their black ties and cowboy boots
would not have foiled the bombs,
but maybe their women's silver embroidered
gowns, jeweled straps, duchess satin coats
could have served as
designer body armor.

and the sky turns red[9]

For Jason Poole

Doesn't remember the explosion,
the days before, the days after,
but he dreams,
again and again he dreams
he's in Iraq and the sky turns red.

His comrades have told him
a bomb went off.
The force of the blast fractured his skull,
injured his brain, one of its major arteries,
his left eye, his left ear.

He was going home in ten days.

After three tours,
he was going home to become a teacher.
He had joined at seventeen
hoping the Marines would help pay
for his education.

And they have.
They have paid for hours and days,
weeks and months, of private tutoring.

They have provided speech therapists
who have taught him to talk.
He still has trouble finding the right words,
and sometimes loses his train of thought.

After months of therapy,
his reading ability has gone from zero
to almost third grade.

---

[9] Based on Grady, Denise. "Struggling Back from War's Once-Deadly
Wounds." *The New York Times,* 22 Jan. 2006.

They have provided physical therapists,
who have taught him to walk,
only, when he crosses a street,
he has to remember to look back
over his left shoulder,
the side where he lost his sight and hearing,
for cars turning right.

Someday he may be able to volunteer
as a teacher's aid,
but with his third-grade reading ability,
he will not be a teacher.

They would pay for his college education,
if he could pass the admissions tests.

The explosion broke every bone in his face,
shattered some, pulverized others.

They have provided him with reconstructive surgeries,
bone grafts, titanium pins to join his bones,
protein implants for his cheek and forehead.

He wanted to marry his sweetheart
when he got back.
With his intact sense of humor,
he says, *But I didn't come back.*

A Promise is a Promise

With his fourth tour of duty
he had fulfilled most of his commitment,
and had told his girlfriend
he wanted to become a teacher
by collecting on that promise of an education.

The government is willing,
but first he must learn to swallow and eat.
The speech therapist is teaching him
with apple sauce and ice chips.

While he waits for his false eye
and his prosthetic leg,
she will teach him to speak,
for now, he responds with a blink.

Someday he will graduate
to recreational therapy,
where he will learn to fit big round pegs
into big round holes
and play a round of Uno,
a game where he will match
numbers and colors.

When his fingers are more nimble
and can pick up the cards,
he will spend months rocking his frustration,
trying to remember *blue*.

for birds don't mourn in darkness

In the darkness of the night,
he comes back,
without a commander-in-chief
to honor his service,
a loved one to cry over his casket,
a countryman to mourn for him,
a dog to whimper for his master.

In the silence of the night,
our young soldier arrives
in a dark pine box and,
like a duffle bag, rolls
down the conveyor belt
on the bottom of the plane,
down he rolls
without sobs,
chants,
laments.

In the still of the night,
he returns
without a funereal bugle,
a heavenly harp,
a song of bird,
for birds don't mourn in darkness.

The Aftertaste

You went out
on the morning roads,
on the lanes jammed
with the thousands fleeing
the missiles and the bombs,
with their blankets and their ovens
and their sacks of flour
for tomorrow's bread
piled on the borrowed trucks,
the white and orange taxis,
the rickety mini-buses.

You left
with the bundle of your clothes,
your Koran, your photos,
the address of the cousin
you hoped would give you shelter,
your husband's prayer beads,
your husband,
who did not survive
his first checkpoint.

You ran
on the roads of the night,
between the high-precision bombs
and the discovery of Saddam in his spider hole,
between the hospitals without medicines
and the morgues without electricity.

You lurked
on the avenues of fear,
loneliness, grief,
survival.

You were lucky to leave.

Now you crouch
on the streets of sorrow,
the paths of the illegal who
walks the phantom alleys,
seeks the shadowy jobs,
avoids the looks of resentment
that follow her in Amman,
Damascus, Cairo.

You will go out again,
a green card
clutched in your hand,
and you will arrive
on the promised land,
the one that invaded yours.

You will learn their language,
hear their epithets,
watch them burn your Koran,
listen to their curses against the invasion
of the new immigrants.

You will dream.
Hundreds of nights you will wake
with the taste in your mouth
of your mother's chai,
with the smell in your nostrils
of your grandmother's, your habibi's, bread.

Thousands of afternoons
you will close your eyes,
you will hear the seagulls on the Tigris,
you will see the sun going down
behind the palm trees.

And each dawn
of the rest of your days
you will see your husband's misty eyes,
you will taste the damask flesh of the fig
on his lips.

You will return.
One day you will return
with the resplendence of the sun
in your gaze,
with the sweetness of dates
on your tongue.

You will go home.

And McDonald's will offer you a hamburger
wrapped in your grandmother's pita,
with an aftertaste of preservatives.

The sun will set behind a Wal-Mart,
and palms will have forgotten their calling,
their fruit will offer you
the bitter taste
of all the moments of your absence.

Army Surplus

Polishing your grandson's shoes,
you remember counting *eight, nine, ten,*
remember sighing with relief,
smiling as your chest expanded
with the fullness of her perfection.

Ten little fingers. Ten tiny toes.
How can nature make something so small
so perfect?

The next day you dressed her all in pink
from her bonnet down to the booties
you crocheted for her trip home.

Your sister bought your daughter's first pair
of white kid leather booties.
They're in the box in the attic
with her christening gown.

Grandma bougt her first pair of white Mary Janes
the summer she turned three.
You bought her first pair of black patent leathers
for her picture with Santa.

Her first day of kindergarten
she came home with a bloody nose
and scuffed Stride Rites.
Dad insisted on having them bronzed.
They sit on his desk in his study.

Will he come out of there today,
go with you?

Oh, and that pair of hideous
high-top purple sneakers
she talked Grandpa into buying--
the beginning of the rebellious teens.

After that, she cut out holes in all her sneakers
and with her babysitting money
bought those clunky motorcycle boots
from the Army Surplus Store.

Would she ever look like a woman?

Then she noticed boys,
and you walked with her
through every department store in town
looking for the perfect prom shoes,
and there she was,
a beautiful young woman
in her emerald silk gown
and her silver sandals.

She chose her own graduation shoes,
too high, too flimsy,
but you kept your mouth shut.

And for her wedding,
a shimmering fantasy on heels
hand-made by her Italian neighbor.

The day you heard she was pregnant
you started crocheting again,
couldn't wait for the sonogram,
crocheted pink, white, blue, yellow, booties.

Today you polish your grandson's good shoes,
he must look nice,
you're taking him to the traveling memorial
that has finally come to town.
You hope Dad comes out of his study,
it has been harder on him.

Still, you want him with you
when you help your grandson
slip the pink booties
you brought down from the attic
inside the army boots
tagged with his mother's name.

Zapaterismo

France and Germany refuse to agree to the invasion,
the Secretary of Defense declares them
"old Europe."

Afraid of associating with anything not hip,
new Americans pour their vintage wine down the tube,
develop a distaste for brie,
turn their noses up at French perfume,
rename their *frites*,
and close down the Statue of Liberty.
If anyone disagrees —how is it possible
not to think like an American?--
he will be demonized.

A commentator says Spaniards are decadent
for holding their president,
the Benjamin of the invasion triumvirate,
accountable for his lies and deceptions,
and voting him out of office.

A fellow in one of the thinking tanks
declares Spain
"old Europe,"
cowardly, and decadent.

Must I now feed my aged Manchego
to new American mice,
pour my Marqués de Cáceres
down the ruse,
burn my *Quijote*,
at the stake of new American patriotism?

The thinking fellow informs us
the Zapateros of Europe cannot be taken seriously.

Spain's new leader is Rodríguez Zapatero,
Rodríquez for his father, Zapatero for his mother,
but to know that would require a bit of curiosity
about old customs,
something not expected of new fellows.

Perhaps the Rodríguez Zapateros of the world
refuse to go along with America's war
because they are old.

They were new empires once.
Maybe they now seek timelessness,
as in the connection of child to parent,
and parent to grandparent,
family to village,
citizen to leader,
bird to tree,
wolf to human,
sequoia to earth,
man to his word,
humility to peace.

That was my pig: A Found Poem[10]

For Petty Officer Third Class Dustin E. Kirby

He flips the empty helmet,
exposes the inside lined with blood and splinters,
bandages the head,
helps load the wounded marine into a helicopter,
then says,

I kept him breathing.
His name was Lance Cpl. Colin Smith.
. . . .
His eyes were O.K. They were both responsive.
And he was breathing.
And he had a pulse.
Smith has been with me since I was...
He was my roommate before we left.
His dad was his best friend.
He's got the cutest little blond girlfriend,
and she freaks out every time we call
because she's so happy to hear from him.
I really thank God that he was breathing
when I got to him
because it means that I can do something with him.
It helps...
It helps, because if he's breathing,
you're doing something

Before deploying,
Doc Kirby took a trauma treatment program
where each student got an anesthetized pig:

You get a pig and you keep it alive.
And every time I did something to help him,
they would wound him again.

---

[10] As reported by Chivers, C.J. "Tending a Fallen Marine, With Skill, Prayer, and Fury." *The New York Times,* 2 November 2006. Dustin E. Kirby was seriously wounded himself on Christmas Day, 2006.

So you see what shock does,
and what happens when more wounds are received
by a wounded creature.

My pig? They shot him twice in the face
with a 9-millimeter pistol,
and then six times with an AK-47,
and then twice with a 12-gauge shotgun.
And then he was set on fire.
I kept him alive for 15 hours.
That was my pig.
That was my pig.
Smith is my friend.

Totenbuchen

> It will take a thousand years for blood to be worn
> away from the charnel house, for the bell tolling
> to reach the last name in the Totenbuch--one thousand
> years too late for the human to be touched with humanity.
>
> —David Ray, "The Perimeters of Grief"

The Egyptians and the Tibetans
had their books of the dead,
spiritual guides for the afterlife.

The Nazis had theirs—
detailed accounts of each prisoner:
name, religion, occupation,
country of origin, marital status,
number of children,
the gold, jewels, paintings, suitcases,
they abandoned
or took to the camps,
who went to the ovens,
who to the showers.

The Americans don't do books.
They don't do body counts either.
Sometimes they don't do bodies.
They just call in air strikes
on the houses where they have shot
insurgent grandfathers in wheel chairs,
insurgent brides,
insurgent babies.

Carding

Women comb hair
till they bleed.
                    —David Ray, "Fascism Again"

Dancing in the street
or alone in their cells,
to kill the devil in their souls
men chant, beat their chests.

With whips, chains, thorns,
they flail,
cover their penance
with stiff hair shirts.

Before their scabs heal,
they flagellate again.

Now women card their hair,
and have no coronet
to cover
their penance.

Each cards harder each day,
for the devil whispers
she could have thrown
her warrior son from the wall.

The Gravedigger[11]

It is as if Saddam had never left.
                    —Sheik Jamal al-Sudani

He buries the dead,
not the infirm who die of old age,
not the sick who succumb to ill health,
not the victims of famine, flood,
or earthquake,
but the ones the whim of a tyrant,
tribal dispute, or ethnic revenge
mark for a bullet in the heart,
a rope around the neck,
bomb fragments in the gut,
a drill hole in the head.

He has devoted his life to
washing and shrouding,
covering with earth
the victims of hate,
the remains that pile up in the morgue,
unclaimed for fear of revenge.

Sometimes, he gets five hundred in a week,
sometimes, only a coarse sack
full of heads.

Tired, but resigned to his fate,
he wraps each in six meters of plastic
and loads it onto a flatbed
for the journey
through the Triangle of Death.

---

[11] Inspired by Jaber, Hala. "Grim days for the gravedigger of Baghdad." *TimesOnLine* (from *The Sunday Times*), 10 September 2006.

At the holy cemeteries of Najaf and Karbala
he washes each body,
assigns it a number,
records moles, scars, other notable marks,
photographs the face,
shrouds it in ten meters of cotton,
lays it in a grave,
sometimes deep enough for the plague,
sometimes just enough for marauding wild dogs.

Olivia

For Olivia Simone Mays

She's three,
and still remembers her mother
pushing her in her blue stroller.

When she sees it in the garage,
she wants to climb in,
go for a ride.

But she's a big girl now,
it's her turn
to push Daddy in his wheel chair
outside the polytrauma center.

A Third Kind

The mutilated rot in their beds, some for the rest of their lives.
So the dead and the mutilated both rot, in different kinds of graves.
    —Harold Pinter, *Art, Truth, and Politics,* Nobel Lecture, 2005.

He lost both arms and his sight.
The blast rattled his skull,
reduced his mental capacity
to that of a child.

Soon his two sons will outpace him.
He will not understand,
but his young wife will.

Three Acts

... it is more important that we remain current on emerging trends in theater.

—Brigadier General Michael D. Barbero, Commandant
Joint Readiness Center and Fort Polk, Louisiana

I. Rehearsal

Exercises in urban operations
imagined by dozens of scriptwriters,
produced by a defense contractor
in a miniature Iraqi city
with Arabic road signs,
mosques with smoke-making machines,
simulated I.E.D.s, booby-trapped dogs, and
recordings of screaming.

The administrator promises to add
the smells of burning bodies and death.

The mock-up city is populated with
Arabic-speaking immigrants to act as civilians,
local pensioners to act as journalists,
soldiers to act as insurgents,
soldiers training for deployment
to act as themselves.

Hits are registered on uniform receptors
that chirp when struck.
A player consults a sealed card to find out
whether he is dead.

The action is recorded by thermal imaging cameras
and satellite positioning technology
so that in the control center
officials sitting in high-back leather chairs
can follow it across maps lit up on giant screens.

II. Performance

-- Break a leg! or *Merde*, as the French say

After graduation,
soldiers deploy to the real-life stage
armed with the most advanced voice communications,
night vision systems,
lethal weapons.

They are protected with bullet-proof vests,
Kevlar helmets, armored vehicles,
$79,000 electronic jammers to defeat explosive devices,
a few, with the $200,000 Warlock.

Soon each soldier learns
that in the city that is not fake,
the play lasts longer,
smoke is produced by bombs,
bullets feel different from laser beams,
he doesn't need a card to tell him he's wounded,
screaming is born of unscripted terror,
crying, of losing a limb that bleeds
without a blood-spurting machine.

In the city that is not fake,
there is no need for an administrator to add
the smell of fuel mixed with gunpowder
and burning flesh.

The troops are accompanied to theater
by state-of-the-art field hospitals
manned by the best-trained surgeons,
as well as by morgues
equipped with an ample supply of bags.

Once stabilized,
a soldier is evacuated to Mosul,
Kuwait, Landstuhl, the States.

III. After the Show

In the States, he goes to Walter Reed, Bethesda,
the new amputation center in San Antonio,
or one of the polytrauma centers built for this war.

If he loses an eye, he will be fitted with a false one.
He will be trained to use his own
personal global positioning system (GPS)
by voice or in Braille.
He can choose software that operates his computer by voice,
or one that reads aloud to him.

If he's an amputee, he will be fitted with
an advanced prosthetic limb,
or two.
If his mind is intact, he can qualify for
a $50,000 limb with microchips.
While in recovery, he can use a cane, a walker,
a wheelchair,
a stair-climbing wheelchair,
a wheel-chair operated with a mouthpiece.

If his skull is crushed, he can have his brain protected
with a metal plate and a padded helmet
until the plate can be replaced with prosthetic bone.

If his face is destroyed, it can be reconstructed
with titanium rods and screws,
with bone and skin grafts.

If he can't breathe, he can have
a cuffed device
installed in his tracheotomy.

If he suffers brain damage,
they will teach him to swallow and eat,
perhaps to walk and talk.

They will give him medication for his headaches,
therapy for his mood swings,
techniques for managing his anger,
group therapy for his substance abuse.

Throughout his months of recovery,
throughout his years of living with diminished capacities,
he will remember his world class training
in the fake Iraqi city of Louisiana,
and he will wish that just one of the props
had not been fake.

He will wish he had a god gun
to erase real wounds,
grow new limbs,
resurrect old buddies.

into the lizard's eyes

For María del Carmen Saen-de-Casas

When they were expelled from Paradise, Adam and Eve moved to
Africa, not Paris.
Sometime later, when their children had gone out into the world,
writing was invented.
In Iraq, not Texas.

—Eduardo Galeano, "Some Forgotten Truths" [12]

I touch the glasses I brought
from across the ocean,
choose the one with the blue-shadowed
white blossoms
that fits just right in my drowsy hand.

As the sun rises over the pecan groves,
in my adobe house in Casas Grandes,
within walking distance
of the rammed-earth buildings
abandoned
more than a thousand years ago
by the original settlers of Paquimé,
I rub the last dream off my eyes
and touch the gold-rimmed tea glass
I bought in El Albaicín,
Granada's Moorish quarter.

Looking out at the autumn sky,
yellow grass, naked trees,
I stare at the lizard
that comes every morning
to gaze at me as I drink my coffee
and prepare for the day's writing.
The steaming milk with espresso
warms my hand,
and I touch, across the window pane,

---

[12] "Algunas verdades olvidadas."

the lizard's pulsating belly,
feel its beating heart,
its tiny, powerful, beating heart
that vibrates her elongated body
and brings her to my window
to start my writing ritual.
As we stare at each other,
her amber gaze stirs old memories.

The sun sets over Sierra Nevada
while in a whitewashed building
along the Darro River,
I sit on a large embroidered cushion
on the floor of a teashop
around a small marquetry table,
holding a shimmering glass,
sipping sweet Alhambra Dreams,
savoring honey-dripping pastries,
listening to Carmen tell Anna,
Jennette, Duke, the young Americans
studying with us in Seville,
about the Alhambra's Nasrid architecture,
the ceiling of Salon of Ambassadors
that represents the seven heavens
of Muslim cosmogony,
the Patio of the Lions,
the fountains and terraced gardens,
the pomegranate trees,
the jasmine fragrance,
the stories of Zoraya's doomed love,
of the thirty-two massacred Abencerrajes,
of Napoleon's attempt
to blow up the red fortress,
of the spot, el Suspiro del Moro,
where the last Moorish king cried
the loss of his Al-Andalus kingdom.

Sitting in one of the cafés
in the portals around
Jardín del Centenario,
half-listening to Mate and Aída
talk about the changes Coyoacán

has experienced through the years,
I look across and see
the palace of the Spanish conqueror
who tortured the last Aztec king,
and hear the blind organ-grinder
playing *María Bonita,*
the same Agustín Lara tune
I used to hear
sitting on my bedroom floor,
peeking through the blinds
at the old man winding his hurdy-gurdy
on the corner of our apartment building
on Marsella Street.

I drop a coin in his bucket
and make my way through the alleys
formed by the book-fair stalls
in the center of the plaza,
stroll through the rows of tables
laden with new and used books,
sheet music, magazines,
language programs,
CDs of classical music,
love ballads, political protest songs,
indigenous instruments,
poems read by their authors,
sung by others.
I touch old favorites,
El arco y la lira, El llano en llamas,
Visión de los vencidos,
Elogio de la sombra,
El silencio de la luna,
Los versos del capitán,
leaf through new ones,
touch the pages,
some still uncut, some crumbling,
look at the old photos,
the handwriting
of letters and manuscripts,
run my fingertips over the faces,
the words, the white spaces,
Soul-Braille of the lover of poetry,

hear the melodies, the rhythms,
the breath,
hear the breath of my favorite poets.

I touch their breaths and their voices,
and my heart shrinks
remembering the ones I will not hear,
the ones I will not touch,
the voices silenced by the bombs
that killed and injured dozens
and destroyed the ancient buildings
of Al-Mutannabi Street,
the historic center
of intellectual and literary life
in the cradle of my civilization,
and I say *my civilization*
for what I love is mine,
even if I have not seen it,
and now, never will.

Of course, those bombs
aimed at the love of the word,
at the word of protest
and the syllables of love,
exploded first,
not in the street of The Poet,
but in the hollow heart of the bomber.

I hear the explosions,
and I touch the flames,
the smoke, the soot, the ashes.
I hear the explosions,
and I smell the blood,
I smell the red blood spurting
and the black ink running
down the booksellers' row
towards the Tigris.

I hear the explosions,
and I touch the grief
for the dozens killed and injured,
for the evil that stokes

a sick man's hunger for destruction.
I touch the grief
for the attacks on our civilization.

I hear the explosions,
and I touch the fear
of the intellectuals and the writers
forced underground,
exiled from al-Shabandar Café,
from Al-Arabia Bookshop,
from the Modern Bookstore,
from the Renaissance Bookstore,
from their meandering alley
of dilapidated Ottoman buildings,
exiled from their Friday rituals
of buying books,
discussing politics, reading poetry,
drinking their sweet tea
from shimmering glasses,
smoking their sweet-smelling tobacco
from silver, crystal, gilded or colored glass
hubble bubble pipes
through the silver mouthpiece they carry
in their pockets,
in case someone has defiled
the amber mouthpiece
with his lips.

I hear the explosions,
and I touch the anger
of the writers and intellectuals
who wander the world
exiled from their booksellers' row,
from their writers' sanctuary,
from their traditions,
from their book-loving culture.

I touch the gold-rimmed tea glasses,
the ornate, antique pipes
with their amber mouthpieces,
the sorrow,
the ashes,

the silence.
I touch the silence and the fear.

And, then, on a smoldering
Roman August morning,
when breathing becomes difficult
and clay bakes on the sidewalk,
I touch hope.

Across a Vatican glass case,
I touch the triangular shaped symbols
made by a stylus on wet clay
that was later baked into a rose-colored
inscribed and sealed envelope
for a dark grey cuneiform tablet
from the Old-Babylonian Period,
circa 1700 B.C.
I touch a pink tablet,
Number IV of the Poem of Erra
from the New Babylonian Period,
circa 629-539 B.C.
I touch a grey cylinder
divided into three columns
celebrating the reconstruction
of the Temple of the god Lugal-Marda.
It dates from the New-Babylonian Period,
reign of Nabuchadnezar II,
circa 605-562 B.C.
I touch a legal document
from the Ur II Period,
circa 2100-2004 B.C.

I touch mankind's first writing,
invented in Iraq
over five thousand years ago,
and I know that no bomb
will ever destroy
man's need to leave a written record
of his sorrows, of his loves,
of his triumphs and losses,
of his enduring struggle
to construct a world of respect,

respect for humans,
respect
for the clearest manifestation
of the human.

Back in my adobe house,
near the rammed-earth city
abandoned
more than a thousand years ago,
for reasons we don't understand
because their builders left us
no written history,
Eduardo Galeano reminds me,
from Montevideo,
via a Buenos Aires internet journal,[13]
that a few centuries
after the invention of proto-cuneiform
in Mesopotamia,
mankind's first love poem was written,
in Sumerian, by Enheduanna,
daughter of Sargon, King of Akkad,
and high priestess of Nanna,
the moon god.

Her poem of a night of passion
between Innana, goddess of Love,
Sexuality, and Fertility,
and the shepherd Dumuzi,
was written on wet clay.

Her hymns to the goddess
are the first poems written
in the first person
and signed by a poet conscious
of her relationship to the goddess.

Looking into the lizard's eyes,
watching her soft, pulsating belly,
I touch faith,

---

[13] *Gaceta Literaria Virtual,* octubre 2008. Dirección Norma Segades-Manías.

faith that in Mesopotamia,
Uruguay, Tenochtitlán,
or Texas,
in the end will be the word,
the human word of lament,
the human howl of injured justice,
the weeping of sorrow,
the cry of desolation,
the whisper of compassion,
the invocation of the truth,
the proffering of forgiveness,
the melody of love,
even if it has to be scratched
on scorched earth.

The Human Switch

Every Marine needs to have a "human switch." When you go to war, you have to be able to switch it off. "If you're in a situation where you have to kill, then you kill everything —women, children, plants, dogs— everything, everything. And if you don't do that, you're going to get killed."

—Sargeant Tim Foley quoting his senior drill instructor[14]

[14] Buchanan, Christopher. "A Reporter's Journey: In the tragic story of Marine Lance Cpl. Jeff Lucey and his ordeal in Iraq, what really happened?" *The Soldier's Heart. Frontline*, 1 March 2005. http://www.pbs.org/wgbh/pages/frontline/shows/heart/lucey/

The Human Switch

For Jeff Lucey

The longer you spend in war, the more deformed you become,
and the harder it is to return to a society not at war,
until finally death itself comes as a kind of release.
                    —Chris Hedges, "The Collective Madness"

When Jeff got home,
he told his parents he heard voices,
felt hands on him,
saw faceless old people,
a fox's head walking behind.

He told his father a voice shouted
Pull the fucking trigger,
and as he looked into the eyes
of the scared Iraqi,
wondering if he was somebody's son,
somebody's friend,
the voice again shouted
Pull the fucking trigger.

He shot the young man in the eye,
another, in the throat,
watched them die.

He wrote his girlfriend he committed
so many immoral acts
he just wanted to erase that time,
pretend it didn't happen.

Fourteen months after his return,
Jeff hanged himself with a garden hose.

One of his comrades thinks
just being in a war zone
makes you understand
you could take another's life,

and this may have led Jeff to imagine
the crimes they say
he could not have committed.

Every time the convoy went out,
the commander reminded them,
If somebody, man, woman, or child,
tries to step in front of a truck,
hit him. Crush her. Run them over
like "bumps in the road."

Were the visions of children shot,
women raped,
men sodomized,
of Iraqis considered *bumps in th road,*
enough to make him think
he committed those crimes?

Did he forget to turn off his human switch?

Desert Boots

After Vincent Van Gogh and Martin Heidegger

In the weight of their tired hides,
dust of the desert,
scratches of sand,
cracks of cloudless summer sun.

In the darkness of their mouths,
stench of sweat,
weariness of fear,
feet yearning to go home.

In the thickness of their soles,
the réflex of the occupier,
the master's swagger,
unable to feel the earth,
walk in others' shoes.

In the steel toe,
the women's door kicked open,
the holy objects stomped,
the fingers crushed,

the leash on the naked prisoner,
the Muslim dog,
the grin next to the body
in the black bag.

Crucifixion Update

I

It is a Christ-like figure
with bare feet on a box,
instead of nailed to a cross,
with arms stretched out,
hands attached to electrodes,
instead of nailed to a cross.

A sackcloth with a hole for his neck,
instead of a loincloth,
covers his manhood.
Does it also cover
the marks of the flogging,
does it leave the sides open,
to make room for the spear?

On his head,
a hood,
instead of a crown of thorns,
hides his face,
denies his name,
obscures his pain.

II

A commentator suggests
the figure has become an icon,
a symbol of America.

The world knows
the figure is a symbol of the world,
that it has already drunk wine
mingled with gall,
that it now stands hooded on a box
with electrodes on hands, feet, genitals,
while America the centurion
mocks
spits
casts lots for its robe.

They walk among us

I'm not going to address the torture word ...
>   —Secretary of Defense Donald Rumsfeld

They walk among us,
pass unnoticed,
may live next door,
share our bed,
be our brothers,
our sons.

They look normal,
like you and me,
but don't look in their eyes,
they will lower their lids,
remember the past,
miss the slow, deliberate, pain,
the slow arousal,
water boarding,
punching,
kicking,
cuffing, shackling, pretzeling
bodies
hanging from walls,
doors,
four hours, ten,
all day, night.

Don't ask them to look at you,
they're looking inward,
wishing they were still there
hearing the barking,
enjoying the fear in dark eyes,
the cringing,
the shrinking of manacled limbs
as dark eyes hear panting,
sense steaming breath.

They see themselves there
feeling a slow arousal,
enjoying the pain in dark eyes
when canine eye teeth
cut through glistening skin,
seeing hot golden urine
and warm sticky blood
running down legs,
watching the panic
in dark eyes that fear
they, your neighbor,
your husband,
will let go of the leash,
and they not able
to lower their hands.

Oh, please don't ask them to tell you,
they don't want to scare you,
don't want you to judge them,
don't think you will know
how they were following orders,
trying to please their superiors,
proving they were good freedom soldiers,
defending you and your way of life.

They will not tell you
how forcing the hajis and the ragheads
to masturbate
in front of each other
enduring the looks,
the snickers,
of pretty female soldiers
pointing at their dark erections
satisfied their need
for humiliation,
but soon aroused their desire
for the female soldiers,
for the dark erections.

Don't ask them,
they will not tell you
that everyday life
is no longer enough,
that husbands and wives
are pallid replacements
for the heat and excitement
of arousal
in the midst of barking,
black body bags,
heaps of hooded men
naked in dark lustrous skin,
women in camouflage pants,
velvety boots,
dangling cigarettes.

They don't want to hurt you,
to tell you
arousal is now mingled
with pain in dark eyes,
barking and snarling,
and thinking the other
a dog.

No, they will not tell you
arousal is slow,
and it is heightened
with photos and videos
that keep running on.

They walk among us,
but don't look in their eyes,
they lower their lids,
see themselves there,
put their hands in their pockets
for fear they will disobey,
see themselves there,
wish you were not here.

No! Not my son!

Democracy assassinated the family that was here
—graffiti on a Haditha house

Your son could not have done it,
your boy is not a murderer,
but you have seen the pictures,
the large and the small bundles
wrapped in flowered blankets,
colorful rugs,
the bodies on the trucks,
on the floor of the morgue,
the little girl cross-legged
on the ground
between the blood-splattered wall
and her uncle's bare feet,
the girl who hugs herself,
shoulders stooped,
gaze of terror,
mouth open,
screaming,
mouth that is the scream,
girl who is the scream,
scream whose name is Eman Walid Abdul Hamid,
scream that lives because she hid under the bed,
arms tight around Abdul Rahman, her little brother.

You have read that in the house next door
thirteen-year-old Safa Younis,
covered in her mother's blood,
pretended to be dead,
when the Americans left,
she held her little brother Mohammed
until he died.

You have seen,
you have read,
you have heard,
you want to scream,
No! Not my son!

You will have months to sit in a courtroom,
listen to the horror,
wait,
hope,
pray.

You will have years to visit him in jail,
take him brownies, magazines, cigarettes
leave early because there's nothing to say.

You will have
all the days of your life
to ask yourself what happened.

He's a stranger.
Did you hold him,
your arms tight around him?
Did you kiss him good night?
Did you speak against the war?
Should you have pushed him to flee,
taught him to question,
resist his friends' pressure,
his leaders' lies,
the media's rah, rah, rah?

Did you?
Were you gentle with him?

The Missing Flowers

I look at the photos that have circled the globe
as icons of America's decadence.
I look, and I stare,
and I realize it's not prurience
that holds my attention,
not even surprise,
for when the President said
that we are the good guys,
with God on our side,
and the others are bad,
I knew that horror would follow Empire.

It's not even the natural human recoiling
from cruelty
that keeps me glued to the images,
rather, it is fascination
with the creative impulses
that moved the soldiers at Abu Ghraib,
for, ignoring the blood-splattered walls,
the semen-filled mouths,
the dangling cigarettes,
the executioner's blue gloves,
the grinning and leering and taunting,
and the thumbs-up,
I focus on the centerpiece.

It's the pyramid of naked bodies
that reminds me of art.
I doubt if any of the soldiers,
generals, intelligence experts,
civilian contractors,
or even the Secretary of Defense,
has majored in art,
much less been to the Prado
to study the triptych,
and yet, they all seem intent
on staging Hieronymus' paradise.

Of course, the strutting president
and the boundless narcissism of Empire,
with their shameless lies
and Armageddon fires,
had already staged the torments of hell
depicted in the third panel,
with its burning skies,
carnal mutilation,
nightmarish religious pigs,
and lie-vomiting,
gold-coin-excreting naked asses.

But The Garden --the earthly delights
that will at last convince Islam
of the superiority of Judeo-Christian civilization--
was missing,
so our soldiers decided to complete the triptych.

They had the rough, branch-like,
animal hands
that encircled a woman's torso,
reaching for her breasts,
and, as in the central panel,
they went bareback-riding.
They did not have horses
or tigers or goats or wild pigs,
or stallion-sized birds,
so they made do
with the only four-legged creatures they had
—the prisoners entrusted to them.

Our soldiers rode the prisoners,
and softened them,
making them pliant and docile,
and once in a while, dead.
They even hooded them to look like
Hieronymus' birds.

Though they may not have studied art,
our soldiers have an instinct for drama.
They know sodomy is part of pan erotic lust,
one of the garden's delights.
They did not have a flute,
as Bosch did,
so they substituted broom sticks and chemical lights,
and, for added fascination,
poured phosphoric liquid on their mounts.

Our soldiers, our poor soldiers,
know of the fauna of Eden,
but they had only dogs,
so dogs they used to frighten the prisoners,
even draw blood from them.

And as Empire is superior,
our soldiers decided to outdo Bosch,
so, to the central panel they added
punching and head slamming
and wiring of parts,
cardiac arrests, and icing of bodies.
Our good soldiers,
with their dramatic instinct,
knew how to stage
the Garden of Empire.

It is regrettable, though,
that no one had been to the Prado
to study the triptych,
for they would have known
that in the original
no one wears latex blue gloves
or uniforms,
that democracy underlies
the orgiastic return to the origins,
and that they should have shown us
their own naked asses.

Our soldiers, our good soldiers,
would have known,
had they studied art
or been to the Prado,
that their panel was missing
harps, flutes, and flying fish,
cherries and strawberries,
black-bird-spewing asses,
and flowers blooming from ass holes.

Mirth

The soldier was laughing.

In the wedding video,
all in white, the bride
arrives in her bridal car.

Inside a large goat-hair tent,
men and their sons
relax on colorful pillows,
smoke a water pipe,
finger worry beads,
while young men sway
to the sounds of tribal music.

General Mark Kimmit insists
the site was a legitimate target,
a suspected safe house
for foreign fighters.

There was no evidence of a wedding:
no decorations,
no musical instruments,
no large quantities of food...
There may have been some kind of celebration...
Bad people have celebrations too.

A video shot by AP cameramen
the following day
shows the bride and groom,
guests, musicians,
pots and pans,
fragments of musical instruments,
fourteen dead children,
pieces of ordnance with US markings.

After the bombing,
says a survivor,
American soldiers drove into the village
shooting low on the ground,
targeting us one by one,

I fell into the mud,
my youngest, alive, next to me.
A soldier kicked me.
I pretended to be dead.
The soldier was laughing.

and garlic too?

For Addie Hall

Isn't it foolish of us to expect that the war zone
will not follow a soldier home?
                    —paraphrase of Greg Palast's interview for *Blather*

They thought he was sweet,
could not believe it
when he leapt from the eighth floor
of the Omni Royal Orleans.

A note in his pocket said
he was paying with his life
for the one he took.

For twelve days,
while he spent fifteen hundred dollars
on booze, women, and drugs,
his girlfriend waited for him
in their apartment
above the Voodoo Spiritual Temple.

They found her charred head
in one pot on the stove,
her hands and feet in another,
her arms and legs in the oven,
on turkey-basting trays,
and in the fridge, in a plastic bag,
her torso.

On the counter, next to the stove,
were sliced carrots and potatoes.

In his note,
the decorated veteran confessed
he had twenty-eight cigarette burns
on his body,
one for each year of his life,

to mark his failures as student, worker,
husband, lover, father, soldier.

A fellow bartender says
when Zach drank
he would be haunted
by an overseas incident
involving a child.

In his note he explained,
*I scared myself
not by the action of calmly
strangling
the woman I've loved
for one and a half years...
but by my entire lack of remorse.*

... *until it stops fluttering*

I-It, in contrast, is the typical subject-object relationship
in which one knows and uses other people and things
without allowing them to exist for themselves in their uniqueness...
—Martin Buber, *I and Thou*

The US government has told the world
that they are bad,
the worst of the worst.

It has told them
they will be in Guantánamo
forever,
without any rights,
not even the right to die.

When they get depressed,
the government mocks them.
When they attempt suicide,
it accuses them of asymmetrical warfare.

When they go on hunger strikes,
it immobilizes them on metal chairs,
pins their ankles, waists, wrists,
shoulders, heads,
then forces flexible feeding tubes
through their nostrils,
down their throats,
into their stomachs.

Dr. William Winkenwerder,
architect of the force-feed policy,
says,

Our intentions are good.
We are seeking to preserve life.

Preserve life obeisant
behind barbed wire,
chained to a forced-feeding chair.

Preserve life,
as when a man beats his wife,
then rushes her to the emergency room,
she has no right to die,
she is his.

Preserve life because the jailer,
as the husband,
needs the abject piece of meat
he beats every day.

Preserve life
as in the art of preserving a butterfly
by trapping the specimen in a net,
immobilizing it
with a gentle pinch on the thorax,
placing it in an extermination bottle
until it stops fluttering,
transporting it to the mounting place
in a relaxing box,
for easy manipulation
the butterfly must be relaxed,
pinning its head and thorax on a board,
spreading its wings, legs, antenna,
gluing its wings,
drying, labeling, storing it,
sitting back to enjoy
being the owner of
a butterfly preserved.

Soldier's Heart[15]

For U.S. Marine Rob Sarra

For my enemy is dead, a man divine as myself is dead,
I look where he lies white-faced and still in the coffin
-- I draw near,
Bend down and touch lightly with my lips
the white face in the coffin.
> —Walt Whitman, "Reconciliation"

All in black,
a bag under her arm,
she walks towards the convoy
at the edge of Ash Shatrah.

The marines hold their arms up,
yell at her to stop.
She walks on.
They raise their weapons,
she keeps walking.

Afraid she's a suicide bomber,
the sargeant aims,
his men aim too.
With fifteen weapons they shoot.

As she falls,
she's reaching into her bag.
When she hits the ground,
there's a white flag in her hand.

The sergeant tries to convince himself
this is something that happens in war,

---

[15] Based on Burke, Thomas. "Interview." *The Soldier's Heart. Frontline*,
1 March 2005.
http://www.pbs.org/wgbh/pages/frontline/shows/heart/interviews/bur
ke.html

decides not to tell anybody,
doesn't want his mother to know
he shot a civilian woman.

When he gets home,
he drinks and gets into fights
until one night he comes to
holding a stranger in a chokehold,
his buddy trying to convince him to let go.

When the stranger goes limp,
he realizes he almost killed a man.

In World War I they called it shell shock,
in World War II, battle fatigue,
since Vietnam, post-traumatic stress disorder.

Perhaps the most appropriate name
for the nightmares, flashbacks, panic attacks,
soldiers suffer when they have caused a death,
is the one used during the Civil War.

Soldier's Heart speaks to the essence,
for a soldier's heart knows
that when he has taken a life,
the furies will haunt him
until he remembers that his enemy
is a man as divine as himself.

... *but this is a birdless zone*

Combat provides a peculiar and deadly thrill,
even as it rewires the brain and unleashes the nightmares.
—Andrew Himes, "Hell-fire and Transcendence"

With drums and trumpets
and the tears of loved ones
they march off to defend goodness.

With the promise
they will be welcomed as liberators,
their courage rewarded with sweets and flowers
and the song of birds,
their return celebrated
with drums and trumpets,
and the kisses of mothers and wives,
and the smiles of new sons,
they march off to battle darkness.

By dawn and by dusk
they see their friends blown to dust
by people who yearn to be free of them,
by the careless acts of commanders,
by their own hand.

And they lie awake
listening to bombs and screams,
not knowing when they will be next.

In the dark and in the light
they see their comrades kill and maim
the sons and daughters of the men and women
they came to liberate.

They shoot and they bomb
because they fear the darkness.

And they lie awake and wonder
when their best friends will liberate
the barbarians in their souls,
start hanging ears around their necks
as their fathers did in Nam,
or kill their wives,
as their comrades did
on their return from Afghanistan.

They lie awake and wonder
if the darkness is in them,
then go home and hear
the whispers and the shouts
and the drumming thunder of regret,
and the voices of their leaders
who call them cowards
because they did not take
killing
in their stride.

They go home and listen
to the silence of the birds,
and the soldiers of the waning hearts
know it's time to listen to the evensong.

Waiting for the Barbarians

Jackals that the jackals would despise
stones that the dry thistle would bite on and spit out,
vipers that the vipers would abominate.

—Pablo Neruda, "I'm Explaining a Few Things,"
Tr. Nathaniel Tarn.

and the stars do not want it

... and the Pentagon did not spin off
into the stars and the war went on
for a few more years.

—David Ray, "Levitating the Pentagon"

David reminds us that in the Sixties
protesters chanted in front of the Pentagon,
hoping to levitate it,
send it off into space
to rid the earth of its evil.

They did not know the stars do not want it,
that intelligent life in the universe
has a shield against earth's evil.

The Pentagon, it seems,
is on the only planet
that can bear it.

Concerto Grosso

Tucson, 2003

Eleven o'clock, warring hour,
my move to the city accompanied
by the roar of the helicopter.
They fly south, west, north,
two, three, four, in a row,
turn east, south, west,
time after time, hours on end.

Some nights one rotates
over my roof,
changes the pitch of the rotor blades,
reminds me of the rusty In-Sink-Erator
needing replacement,
then flies sideways,
pirouettes,
hums and hovers in my head,
spins my paranoia--
they know my name, are
checking on the e-protests and
impeachment petitions I've signed.
I'll spend my dotage in Guantánamo.

Davis-Monthan has apologized,
explained it as military maneuver,
preparedness training for Iraq,
Pakistan, Afghanistan,
all the cubbyholes of the earth
where terrorists lurk,
stockpile weapons.

Dissident alien weirdo that I am,
it doesn't make me feel secure.

As former military wife,
I know American soldiers are not
ten-feet-tall heroes with foot-long
phalluses--they just think they are.

The uniform adds inches,
the armor, the M-14,
the Bradley, or the Apache,
manly valor.

One night,
a whimper outside my bedroom
startles me.
Has someone abandoned a helpless infant?

The pitiful cry alternates with silence,
becomes lament,
returns to whimper.
Sigh of relief--it's not
a suffering baby.
But the mournful call is three nights long,
more disturbing than the roar of the helicopter.

Annoyed with insomnia,
I feel sorry for her discomfort,
angry at the neighborhood tomcats
musking their territory,
filling my open garage,
my laundry area,
with their testosterone stench.

At night,
they draw a perimeter
around the house.
When dawn comes,
their essence wafts in through closed doors,
but where are they on whimpering nights?
What do they do with their strutting maleness?
Do they need a uniform or a bayonet
to answer the call?
Are they being obstructionists?

Or has the roar of the helicopter lowered
feline testosterone,
its gas fumes altered
the rhythms of life?

In the morning,
a pheasant strolls down Helen Street,
looks right, left,
with measured steps, crosses Norton Avenue,
a tourist in a strange land,
uncertain,
in silence.

Marabunta

The cost of the soldier in the field is so high, both in cash and in a political sense that robots will be doing wildly dangerous tasks [in battle in the very near future].

—Colin M. Angle, co-founder of iRobot

Robots in battle will soon look and move like
crickets, cockroaches, hummingbirds,
even swarms of "smart dust."

Why insult the crickets,
the hummingbirds,
the dust?

Better to make robot soldiers in the image
of the dollar sign,
and, if we must insult an animal,
hyenas, or swarms of locusts.

Pink Alert or Happy Is the Color of Subversion

For Cindy Sheehan and Medea Benjamin

> On a wall in a Madrid eatery hangs a sign that says: No Singing.
> On a wall in the airport of Rio de Janeiro hangs a sign that says:
> No Playing with Luggage Carts.
> Ergo: There are still people who sing, there are still people who play.
> —Eduardo Galeano, "Window on Prohibitions"

Black is for mourning,
but don't mention that.
Corpses come home at midnight
and burials with orphans in black
are not allowed in the news' light.

Red is for danger
and death.
Your son's blood was drained in the sand,
but in his casket he looks almost alive.
So don't think of blood,
for you should remember that red is for danger.

Orange means warning of danger,
your leaders must warn you
and warn you.
They would be remiss
if they didn't remind you of
al-Qaida and terrorist cells
and people with turbans and veils,
Saddam and Iran, Korea and its bomb,
explosives in heels, and nail files in bags,
white powder in letters,
uranium from Niger,
and mushroom-shaped clouds.

They would be remiss
if they didn't dress in orange jump suits
the worst of the worst,
the dangerous men they picked up abroad,

and rendered to Cuba and hid behind wire,
and labeled with logic that's razored
and words somewhat oranged.

Yellow means wait,
wait, and keep waiting,
for tomorrow is sure to be orange or red.

And while you are waiting, you must also worry.
If you do not fret, then you're un-American,
and we need to warn others about you.

Pink is for babies and peonies and roses,
and the soft cheeks of children,
and the radiance of lovers.
The sky can betray a suggestion of pink
for a moment at dawn,
and magnolias give just a hint of its softness
before they display their blossoms and brightness.

You wouldn't think anybody could turn
the beauty and joy, the becoming of pink
into perfidious offenses,
but when four middle-aged women in pink
tried to deliver a petition for peace
to the US Mission in New York,
they were handcuffed, dragged to a wagon,
and locked in The Tombs,
a jail full of felons and roaches.

They were charged with trespassing,
disorderly conduct, resisting arrest,
and obstructing
the administration of government.

At their trial months later, Mission staff,
security guards, police officers,
and various and sundry patriots
declared the women's plan to get arrested
a publicity stunt.

Richard Grennell,
the head of communications for the Mission,
professed he perceived the women as threat
for they were dressed in pink,
and laughing,
and singing "Give Peace a Chance," and
they were... they were...
they were clearly happy.

Dynasty

For Edward C. Spencer

Bush bombed Iraq.
His first born bombed it again.
Will the future thank the son
for having only daughters?

A Small Red Blotch

For Omar Khadr and Mohammed Jawad

Maybe this is the last time we will dance.
—One of the 139 girls abducted from St. Mary's College
by the Lord's Resistance Army

I

The abductors' guns and machetes froze her mind,
liquified her body,
made her unable to change into a dress, slip on shoes.

Abducted from her convent in the night,
Grace spent the next seven months
walking through the bush,
barefoot,
still in her nightgown.

They told her and twenty-nine of her classmates
if one escaped, the others would die.

Initiated with a beating,
she was ordered to kill a younger girl,
clean and dismantle guns,
abduct other children,
be a wife to the rebel commanders.

She was fifteen.

When his friends' feet swelled,
and they couldn't walk,
Christopher was forced to club them to death.

It was his initiation into the Lord's Resistance Army.

For the next nine years
he burned huts, sliced off lips,
pounded newborns in wooden mortars.

At eighteen, he says,
I killed, and killed, and killed,
now I'm scared of myself.[16]

II

In the United States,
children are allowed to grow until they're seventeen.
Their bodies are not carried off in the middle of the night,
and their commanders need no guns or machetes
to abduct their minds when they turn thirteen.

When the Senate asked for aggressive,
innovative experiments to find new soldiers,
the Army designed *America's Army,*
a state-of-the-art on-line video game to teach children
about the excitement of military life.

It spared nothing to make it realistic,
with 3-D graphics, surround sound,
and the most advanced gaming technology.
Its combat simulator is a training ground
for real combat,
with real-time reloading clips,
the explosion of different types of grenades,
guns that malfunction from time to time,
night-vision goggles that make the exact click and whir,
even calling the enemy *terrorists.*

But realism has its limits.
In the army's adventures
there is no mention of rape, torture, or civilian deaths.

---

[16] Quoted in Brown, DeNeen L. "A Child's Hell in the Lord's
Resistance Army." *The Washington Post,* 10 May 2006. See also
Gettleman, Jeffrey. "Uganda Peace Hinges on Amnesty for Brutality."
The New York Times, 15 September 2006; Hodes, Jacob and Emma
Ruby-Sachs. "'America's Army' Targets Youth." *The Nation,* 23 August
2002, and Clarren, Rebecca. "Virtually dead in Iraq." *Salon.com,* 16
September 2006.

In 3-D graphics,
a virtual soldier does not look into the eyes
of an unarmed teenager his comrade shoots by mistake,
or for fun.

With surround sound
a virtual soldier does not hear the howl of a mother
whose baby's leg is blown off.

The latest gaming technology
does not reproduce the smell of corpses rotting,
faces melted away,
flesh burned to the bone.
Army's adventures do not show
realistic prostheses or anguished regret.

Virtual soldiers do not say
I am scared of myself.

They die when a small red blotch,
silent,
painless,
appears on the screen.

The Army requires a teen rating for its game.
It needs to catch the attention of virtual soldiers
when they are less than seventeen,
teach them that war is fun,
death, a small red blotch.

Bulletproofing

Traumatic brain injury is the signature wound of this war.
> —Lt. Col. Rocco Armonda, neurosurgeon at
> the National Naval Medical Center

Level I

Wear the standard helmet
your government issues you.
It offers good ballistic protection.

Please be aware that your head
is much more susceptible
to blunt trauma
than your body.
Any impact of a bullet on a helmet
will cause injury and can cause death.

You improve your odds
with head protection,
but no guarantee of invulnerability
can be made.

Level II

BulletProofMe Body Armor Company
recommends
that you upgrade your helmet
with their Foam Impact Liner,
or, better still, upgrade to the
Advanced Combat Helmet
or the Modular Integrated
Communications Helmet,
their interior pad system
offers outstanding comfort
and blunt trauma protection,
or you can just convert
your old standard
to the new Modular Integrated
with a comfort pad system.

Level III

Thank your parents
for paying for your education,
get a scholarship,
or work your way through college.

Do not let the armed forces
promise you an education
after you complete
your obligation to them.
It will be challenging
to attend classes in a wheel chair,
difficult to listen with a hearing aid,
take notes with a prosthetic hand,
concentrate with a pounding headache,
learn with a damaged brain.

Level IV

Choose a blue-blooded family
to be born into.
If your ancestors made their fortune
in steel, tobacco, banking,
oil, armaments, pharmaceuticals,
you will have no need of a helmet.

No need to have to consider
its weight,
side ear coverage,
pre-drilled front hole
for night vision goggle mounting,
whether it has a 2-, a 3-,
or a 3/4-point chinstrap,
or the circumference of your head.

For even if they don't make
a helmet small enough for you,
you will have the wealth,
the connections,
the pedigree,

to get deferments,
get elected, or appointed,
start a war,
and send others to battle
wearing their standard issue,
bubbling with excitement
to spread democracy,
start a new round
of arsenal building.

The Littlest Recruit

21 May 2006

For William Deem

I

A Time of Remembrance,
a celebration to honor the sons and daughters
of the soldiers fallen in Iraq,
and the descendants of the soldiers
of all the wars since the American Revolution,
was organized by a White House Commission.

They invited generals, diplomats,
former prisoners of war,
and orphans.

They planned for singing,
talks of freedom and sacrifice,
and tears.

They planned for children,
and shiny golden medals.

William,
a beautiful, red-haired child of four,
filial pride and ancient sadness in his eyes,
holds, with two little hands, the medal
the Chairman of the Joint Chiefs of Staff
handed him
in honor of his father.
He holds it up
and shows it to his new friend,
an older, dark-haired boy of six.

II

His father was found dead in his bunk
less than a month after arriving in Iraq.
His longstanding depression and anxiety
deepened when his unit was called up.
To handle his heightened stress
the military psychiatrist gave him
a year's supply of antidepressants.

The Army determined
the cause of death was
an enlarged heart complicated by
"elevated levels of Prozac,"
and classified his death as "natural."

III

The White House Commission
didn't plan
for substitute fathers,
only for orphans,
medals,
and heightened levels of Prozac.

The American Century

After *One Thousand Years* by David Ray

Violence is the last refuge of the incompetent.

—Isaac Asimov

They asked for one hundred years
to teach the world democracy.

But a century is not nearly enough.
They had to speed up the lesson
with cluster bombs,
drill it with boots on the ground,
reinforce it with bulldozers,
punctuate it with sharpshooters,
test it with concertina wire,
make it palatable with lies.

They should have asked
for one thousand.

Two Flags

Was that a second flag I noticed
on the President's lapel
on his recent press conference?
I haven't slept since,
trying to decipher its meaning.

After 9/11, he instituted the lapel flag
as symbol of American patriotism.
The next day all Republicans sported one.
Like the Nazi arm band,
no one dares go out in public without a lapel flag,
but what is the symbolism of the second one?

Two is better than one?
My lapel is big enough for Texas-sized patriotism?
Mine is bigger than yours?

Do lapel flags work like emblems of military rank,
tattoos of street gangs,
codes of secret societies?

Did he earn the second one by capturing Saddam?
Will he get a third one for Osama?
Does each flag stand for a country destroyed?

Does each have a specific value—
ten thousand
or a hundred thousand
foreign thugs killed?
So many tons of fire power wasted?
So many pieces of military hardware burned,
making room for the next round of armament building?
Are women and children worth more than armed men--
or less?

Perhaps I am paranoid,
and the little piece of metal on the President's lapel
is only the wire through which

his Vice-President or National Security Adviser can
whisper the answers,
or there is an innocent explanation,
like owning stock in the lapel flag company.

Or are my eyes playing tricks on me, and
instead of a flag I saw a lapel Bible?
A lapel Constitution? A Bill of Rights?
A Patriot Act I, or II?
Is it a casket? A flag-draped lapel casket?
A lapel prosthesis?

Is he hoping that, from a distance,
the flags look like medal ribbons?

Still, I am of the opinion that the President
should appoint a Secretary of Semiotics to his cabinet,
for if it takes two flags to signify patriotism,
then the signs have undergone a devaluation,
and one becomes a symbol of patriotism indecisive,
of resolve in need of steroids
or Viagra.

Does it matter which is on top,
or on the right?
Does one cancel the other like algebraic minuses?
Are they an abacus with a decimal point value?

Or am I missing the point and lapel flags
like talismans,
possess magical powers?

Do they work like the fingers
children cross behind their backs
when they tell a fib,
then affirm,
Cross my heart and hope to die?

Regardless, I do not wish to be unfair.
Maybe there is only one American flag
on the President's lapel,
and the other is Israel's.

Waiting for the Barbarians

Response to Constantine Cavafy

Why did our emperor wake up so early?
He did not sit in state
in the city's grandest gate
wearing his crown, sitting on his throne,
ready to receive the leader of the barbarians.

He heard they were coming
but did not wake up so early
to receive them, for
he had his bicycle to ride
and his underbrush to whack.
He had to keep in shape
and needed to relax.

He had heard the barbarians were on their way,
and did not want them to arrive,
so he sent the young ones of the realm
to fight them on their turf,
flew them over forests, hills, and vales
and across the oceans, deserts, and frontiers
to bomb the barbarians
and haul them off to Abu Ghraib.

Their leader, he was not coming,
he was sitting in state
in his city's grandest gate,
wearing his crown, sitting on his throne,
waiting for the barbarians.

Legacy

We talked through the night,
Steinem, Friedan, de Beauvoir,
César Chávez, Martin Luther King.
Intoxicated with possibility,
we dreamed, signed protests,
sharpened our pencils.

Our daughters would inherit
a tradition of learning and thinking,
become writers, painters, scientists,
take their rightful place in the Academy,
the Cabinet, the Supreme Court.

Three decades after Roe vs Wade,
illiteracy is spreading,
Aids rampant,
the ozone thinning,
children are hungry,
old people, homeless,
and we killed hundreds of thousands
over false intelligence.

We have the Patriot Act, military tribunals,
Enron, Madoff, Halliburton,
the Tea Party,
the oil spill in the Gulf of Mexico,
an imperial presidency.

We did not change the world.

Our daughters have more opportunities.
Some have entered through doors we opened,
some are coming home in coffins and wheel chairs,
leaving our grandchildren behind.

Others choose a white wedding,
a Martha Stewart house,
a uniformed husband,
three sons to send to war.

The Soldier's Words

The soldier says he could
write poems if he wanted to
but doesn't understand
that in the Empire he defends
poetry is high treason
and the words for his pen
are not standard issue.

He didn't see them
flying
the jagged flight
of Baghdad swallows
deafened by the explosions.

He did not sense them
trembling
on the lips of a baby
born by Caesarean
on the eve of the war
so he could flee in his mother's arms
from the menaced city.

He did not hear them
choking
in the throat of the boy
who begged
Water, Mister,
please, Mister, water
when soldiers invaded his village.

He has not heard them
howl
when a man sees his children
blown in front of his eyes
or whimper
when a boy loses his brothers
and both of his arms.

The soldier doesn't know
the words of poems
curse
when a fly alights
on the face of a moribund child,
and gag
with the stench of death
in a ransacked hospital.

He does not know
they are silent
when a soldier sits
on a dirt road
a small body in his arms.

The Murdered

Their mouths are orchards
of lead, singing, and the alleys resound.

—Saadi Youssef, "The Murdered Come Out at Night"
Tr. Khaled Mattawa

The Pied Piper

His face, neck, tie,
background,
all made up of more than
three thousand tiny mosaics.[17]

Did you find your son?
Was he on the forehead,
the lips,
the bridge of the nose,
perched on the lapel flag?

Did you see your mommy?
Was she on his shoulder,
his ear,
his thinning hair?

Did you find your little girl?
Was she near his heart?

The designers tried to help us visualize
the number of Americans
the Rat Catcher had killed.

In those tiny mosaics, Americans saw
the evil of the piper
whose catchy tune they followed.

Today,
with more than four thousand dead,
the mosaics would be smaller,
the faces,
more blurry.

---

[17] See cover of *The Nation,* 24 September 2007. Gene Case and Stephen Kling of Avenging Angels are the designers of this portrait of George W. Bush.

The designers did not include the injured
(more than a hundred thousand),
or the suicides (hundreds each year),
or the wives and girlfriends
the soldiers murder
between tours of duty.

They did not include the Iraqis,
soldiers and civilians,
each of those American soldiers
killed, injured, abused,
before he was wounded
or sent home in a box.
(More than a million).

For a true portrait,
each mosaic of an American soldier
would have to contain,
like a Russian doll,
its own mosaics,
thousands of tiny specs
blending into each other,
barely visible,
of Iraqis and others killed,
maimed, raped, tortured,
orphaned, imprisoned,
impoverished,
exiled,
disappeared.

Even at a microscopic level,
they don't fit.
The murdered don't fit.

Case and Kling will have to design a portrait
that, like a sonogram, shows the inside,
so we can see the microscopic mosaics
that line his skull,
where the dead will feel deader.

But they won't fit there either,
will have to go down into his chest,
find his heart,
touch it.

They will know then
that it was the dead
leading the dead
into war.

The Choicest Flowers

and in the sky
The larks, still bravely singing, fly.
Scarce heard amid the guns below.
—John McCrae, "In Flanders Fields"

With hints of summer,
warm breezes promise long evenings,
days at the beach, the idleness of summer,
the prodigality of life.

Some prepare flower beds,
plant summer vegetables.
Others picnic with friends
while their conversation turns to Little League,
Boy Scout camp,
Martha Stewart's summer desserts,
the neighbors' divorce.

In 1868,
General John A. Logan issued an order
designating May 30th as the day to
gather around their sacred remains
and garland the passionless mounds above them
with the choicest flowers of springtime...

On Memorial Day, we mourn,
but not for long,
for the somber gravity of grief
cannot be sustained
amidst the singing of birds
and the budding of new life
in flowering trees.
A brief moment of sorrow
is aborted
by the unbearable beauty of life.

The choicest flowers of the Civil War
become the red poppies of the Great War,
and the wars continue,
and the battlefields spread,
and the tombs of brave soldiers,
each one someone's son,
each one someone's enemy,
multiply faster than the blooms of spring.

As the deaths of the young increase,
nature rebels, will not supply
enough red poppies for the mourning,
for how many would we need
for the mass graves,
the vaporized, the disappeared,
the graves of enemy soldiers?

A plant in Pittsburgh now makes
the artificial flower of remembrance.
Artificial as the flower is the mourning
and the signing of peace treaties.

We have manufacturers of guns, bombs,
robots, body bags, artificial limbs.
Do we need a factory of peace treaties,
And one of disappearing ink
for the signing of the treaties?

We need to honor dead soldiers,
not as summer with its promise of life abundant
begins,
but on the first of January,
for instead of parades and football jousts,
the rite of winter should be
a remembrance of scarcity, depletion,
life dormant and extinguishable.

A day to remember that a new year
of murdering the young,
aborting life,
desecrating the Earth,

is just beginning.
And if honor the dead we must,
let us go out at dusk,
and in the dying light
place thistles and thorns
on ashen graves.

And if red is the color of mourning,
let us water them with mothers' blood,
for only if women refuse to bear another child
will the factory of death be bare.

The Murdered

But the murdered are replenished. Everyday they are born.
        —Mahmoud Darwish, "Green Flies"

Please tell me about the young men buried in Arlington
and in cemeteries large and small across the land.
Are they the reincarnation of the French and the Americans
interred in Flanders,
the Napoleonic soldiers who lost their lives
to the Russian winter,
or did they last die at Gettysburg?

Did they slaughter the Aztecs at Tenochtitlán?
Did they with Scipio Aemilianus
burn Carthage to the ground?
Did a rain of arrows pierce their hearts at Thermopylae?
Did they go on raids against the Nubians
with King Menes of Memphis?

Are young men, and, now, women, willing to die
for the greed their leaders call freedom,
for the vengeance they praise as honor,
born and reborn,
mere human clay baked in different hues,
trying to use up the karma
they gathered in their previous lives of carnage,
only to accrue new crimes
on their wandering souls' tally?

Are they simple pawns without value,
ready to be played by the masters who win the glory
and cash the prizes?

Is their vocation for anonymous sacrifice
undiminished after each cycle,
born anew with a piranha's ferocity
each time they join a new generation,
die in a different continent?

Is it self-sacrifice, or lust for glory
because they don't understand
how common medals have become,
how in a few years bargain hunters
will get theirs for a dollar
in a flea market?

Or are the dead of all the wars
in all the lands of this earth
virgin flesh, bone, sinew,
fresh blood pumping strong hearts,
readying them to kill and be killed?

Are they first-time-on-this-earth souls,
creatures separate and distinct from all others,
born to replenish the murdered?

And the kings, czars, führers, emperors,
and presidents for life
who send them off to conquer Lebensraum,
stoke their lust for blood,
avenge their fathers,
reclaim their Helens,
assuage their fears of the abyss,
are they all avatars of Wotan,
Ares, Huitzilopochtli?

Are they to be pitied for their deadly drive
to control and accumulate,
for their impotence for life?

Are they interchangeable,
since the more they hate each other,
the more alike they seem?

Do the corporals and the rulers
trade places with each turn of the wheel?

And the woman who gives birth to each,
washes and feeds him,
loves him more than the sun in the sky,
the songbird on her window,

the air in her lungs,
more than her own salvation—
is she willing to raise her son through mumps,
broken bones, all-night fevers,
his puppy's death, his girlfriend's treason,
and then, before he's even a full man,
just hand him over to a chieftain,
an admiral, a tyrant,
knowing her boy will come back
a dead or broken body,
or a soul murdered
for having made of death his whore,
murdered other women's sons?

Can a mother hand her son over
knowing the body that comes back in a coffin
or paralyzed from the shoulders down
carries the unspent seed of his loins,
her murdered grandsons?

Is a mother such an unnatural creature
that she will do what no other beast
on land, air, or water, will—
listen to the fears of old men who have forgotten
that the blood running through a young man's veins
is for begetting, not spilling?

Is she so denatured that she will believe
the lies of a coward
who will not go to battle himself
nor send his own to steal the gold
and the crown of laurel
his shriveled manhood and dusty heart crave,
instead of trusting beyond any ruse or deceit
the life pulsating in her son?

Can a mother do less than the midwives of the Hebrews
who refused to follow the Pharaoh's orders
and found a way to save the men children?

Can she do less than Moses' mother,
who, when she could no longer hide him,
put her baby in a bulrush basket
daubed with slime and pitch
and left him in the sedges by the river's brink?

And if she cannot protect him,
better to throw her son from a wall,
see her infant dead before her eyes
rather than have him come back from war
a wreck who wishes he were dead,
or worse,
a venal ruler
who orders murder on a global scale.

As creation's helpmate,
a woman has the power to withhold.
She can refuse to be a witness to destruction,
tear out her womb
before she will bear the murdered
or the murderer.

Lacrimosa dies illa

Lacrimosa dies illa
Qua resurget ex favilla
Judicandus homo reus.
Huic ergo parce, Deus:
Pie Jesu Domine,
Dona eis requiem.
Amen.

Mournful that day
When from the ashes shall rise
Guilty man to be judged.
Lord, have mercy on him.
Gentle Lord Jesus,
grant them eternal rest.
Amen

On September 11th 2001, like most people around the world, I sat in front of my television watching in disbelief as two planes crashed into the Twin Towers of the World Trade Center and, partially obscured by flames, smoke, and the distance of the cameras, the symbols of capitalism shook and crumbled to the ground.[18] I sat in front of my television for days afterwards, transfixed by the stories of the plane that hit the Pentagon and the one that crashed in a field in Pennsylvania. I listened to the calls the passengers in United Flight 93 and the employees in the burning towers made to their loved ones. I heard countless stories of compassion and heroism, of people who delayed their escape to help a colleague, or a stranger, of the New York police and firefighters who entered the inferno, walked up to the top floors, and led thousands to safety, and of the hundreds who perished when the towers collapsed before they could get everybody out.

For days I watched the images of the planes crashing into the towers, of the more than a hundred people hurtling through space because they chose to jump to their deaths rather than be incinerated, of the hole in the Pentagon wall, of all the forlorn who, like ghosts from the last day of Earth, spent days passing out flyers with their loved ones' pictures, pasting them on makeshift walls, hoping against hope they had escaped and someone knew where they were. I watched all the heart-wrenching images our media played again and again, feeling horror about the cruelty of the perpetrators, admiration for the bravery of those involved in the rescue attempts, sadness for each man and woman who lost someone, for each incomplete family. I spent days and weeks grieving for each child who was left bereft of a father's love, of a sibling's attention, of a mother's care.

---

[18] Many conspiracy theorists believe the way the towers fell, with floors collapsing on each other, was the result of a controlled demolition with pre-installed explosive charges on the structural columns of each floor. They think this crumbling down like a cake is undeniable proof that the attack was the work of the U.S. government, or a joint operation of Israel and the U.S., and that it was done in order to create an excuse to go to war.

For months afterwards, I watched the nightly news filled with pride for the courage of the survivors who spent months in trauma centers trying to heal their broken bones, burned faces, missing limbs, trying to recover from unimaginable injuries to their bodies and their spirits. I was filled with pride for the courage of those who lost a loved one in the attack and, transcending their pain, were able to reach deep into their souls and turn their sorrow into forgiveness. I was touched by the selflessness of the many who travelled great distances, including firefighters from other states, to comb through tons of rubble, ash, and debris for survivors, for artifacts, for the remains of those who did not survive. I was inspired by the countless acts of generosity exhibited by thousands of lawyers, doctors, therapists, podiatrists, clergymen, musicians, and other volunteers, who donated supplies, prepared meals, gave back rubs and foot massages, played music, listened to stories of pain and discouragement, mopped floors, took out the garbage, and, in every imaginable way, created a place of rest and hope for those looking for loved ones and for the thousands involved, first in the rescue attempts, later in the clearance work. This refuge was created in Saint Paul's Chapel, the small 18th-century Episcopal church a few yards from building 5 of the World Trade Center, that miraculously escaped the attacks unscathed. Reverend Lyndon Harris describes the dynamic of this sanctuary as "a reciprocity of gratitude, a circle of thanksgiving—in which volunteers and rescue and recovery workers tried to outdo each other with acts of kindness and love, leaving both giver and receiver changed" ("Sanctuary at Ground Zero").

For months I was filled with pride for the quick and efficient manner in which Ground Zero was cleared and the Pentagon rebuilt. In the months after the attacks, we had Katrina, Haiti, the BP disaster in the Gulf of Mexico, thousands of seriously injured soldiers returning from Iraq and Afghanistan, mix-ups with the graves at Arlington Cemetery, reports of cover-ups when soldiers died from "friendly fire," thousands of veterans homeless or committing murder or suicide, an economy in shambles, and the rich getting richer every day. In the years since then, we have had countless disasters, mistakes, examples of inefficiency, and demonstrations of indifference towards the suffering of others. I have learned that American efficiency, like American generosity, is selective--the efficiency displayed for political or economic motives, the generosity directed towards those who least need it.

Before a month had passed, however, on 7 October, Britain

and the United States, with logistical support from France, Germany, Autralia, and Canada, began bombarding the major cities of Afghanistan. They claimed it was an international campaign to find Osama bin Laden, the mastermind of September 11th, and to punish the ruling Taliban for refusing to turn him over. On 14 October, the eighth day of the bombing, Haji Abdul Kabir, deputy prime minister and the third most powerful figure in the Taliban regime, told reporters that the Taliban would need proof that Osama bin Laden was indeed guilty of the attack, but was willing to turn him over to a third country if the United States ended the bombing. Even before the bombing started, the Taliban had asked for evidence of bin Laden's guilt, and had offered to try him before an Islamic court inside Afghanistan. President Bush said the bombing would not stop unless the Taliban "turn [bin Laden] over, turn his cohorts over, turn any hostages they hold over," and added, "There's no need to discuss innocence or guilt. We know he's guilty" (*Guardian*, "Bush rejects Taliban offer").

Unable to produce proof of his guilt, the United States instead, with the support of the British and other members of the coalition, began a ground invasion, with Northern Alliance forces providing most of the troops. In December 2001, the U.S. and its allies waged an air and land battle in Tora Bora, a cave complex in the White Mountains of Afghanistan, where they claimed bin Laden was hiding in his headquarters. After six days of intensive bombing, they said the al-Qaeda leader had managed to escape into Pakistan. The excuse for the invasion went from capturing bin Laden and destroying his al-Qaeda organization, to punishing the Taliban for refusing to turn him over, to fighting terrorism. From counter- terrorism, the mission evolved into one of nation-building, democratization, and securing rights for women. With the start of the Iraq invasion in March, 2003, the United States transferred soldiers, armaments, and attention to the oil-rich country; Afghanistan was put on a back burner.

A year after the World Trade Center attack, on September 11th 2002, I again spent the day in front of my television watching the memorial ceremonies at the Pentagon, at Shanksville, and at Ground Zero. I watched, and I cried. I cried with the surviving Twin Towers employees, with the police, and with the firefighters who were still grieving for their friends and comrades. I cried with the children in black. I cried with the parents and brothers and sisters and best friends and widows and widowers who were still unable to comprehend their losses.

I was moved by the pomp and circumstance, by the fluttering flags, by the military bands and uniforms, by the reading of the almost 3000 names of those who perished, by the flowers, the vigils, the candles, the music, and by the hundreds of white doves released into many skies of the world. I was moved by the lighting of the Eternal Flame, by the invocations, the readings, and the prayers, by the composers, singers, directors, and musicians who offered their time and passion to compose and to sing and play their spiritual, majestic, music in cathedrals, symphony halls, and city parks all over the world, by the bagpipes, the tolling bells, the ferry horns, the moments of silence.

I was touched by the 3000 white rose petals that fluttered down from the dome at London's St. Paul's Cathedral while a cellist played a Bach suite and the 2000 people in the congregation maintained perfect silence. I was touched by the Quranic prayers for peace, justice, and tolerance offered by Muslim leaders at the Central Mosque in London, by the thousands of motorists in Sydney who turned on their headlights at 8:46 in the morning, by the two towers of light projected into the sky of Paris, by the tree-planting ceremony in New Zealand, by the human stars and stripes flag formed by firefighters and ambulance staff on the beach of Australia's Surfers Paradise, by the Buddhist monks who chanted memorial prayers in front of the U.S. embassy in Tokyo.

I was happy to hear the presidents, prime ministers, ambassadors, religious leaders, and ordinary citizens, from dozens of countries, who observed the anniversary of 9/11 in solidarity with America, condemning the attacks, expressing in almost every human language sorrow for the victims, and declaring a universal desire for healing and global unity. They proclaimed their solidarity for peace, not for revenge, not for eternal war and continuous human suffering.

What moved me the most that day, however, was the *Rolling Requiem*. The traditional Latin Mass for the dead, Mozart's last, great work, left unfinished when he died at the age of 35, was played on the concert stages of London, Sarajevo, Anchorage, New Zealand, and in many cities of the contiguous United States again and again during the months after the attacks. The haunting beauty of the *Requiem* seemed to fill the need we all felt to remember that beauty was still possible in a world filled with cruelty and tragedy.

On the first anniversary of the attacks, following a patron's suggestion, seven members of the Seattle Symphony Chorale implemented the worldwide tribute they spent months organizing. Mozart's *Requiem* was sung by almost 200 choirs in twenty-eight countries and in over twenty time zones representing all seven continents.

Beginning at 8:46 A.M., the time of the first attack on the World Trade Center, west of the International Date Line in Auckland and Wellington in New Zealand and in the South Pole, rolling across each country and around the world from time zone to time zone, and ending in American Samoa, the voices of over 17,000 people rose as a world-wide invocation of hope and healing to honor the dead and give comfort to the living.

The *Rolling Requiem* became for me a symbol of September 11th, not the September 11th of the senseless carnage of 2001, but the September 11th of paying homage to the dead and singing around the earth to heal the losses and the hatreds and to establish solidarity among the living. It became a symbol of the power of music, and of the beauty of human creativity and human understanding. A symbol also of American ingenuity and organization, for it was a group of American women who imagined and executed this amazing first worldwide commemorative event.[19] When the invasion of Iraq began in March of 2003, the *Requiem* was transformed for me into a symbol of opportunity lost, of solidarity betrayed.

What I did not realize at the time, or for many years afterwards, was that it would eventually become a fitting symbol, not of September 11th, but of the Iraq and Afghanistan occupations, of the horrific destruction the United States and its allies have visited upon these two countries and other places of the world, of the Empire's Eternal War. What I did not know at the time was the *Requiem*'s history. Like the Iraq and the Afghanistan invasions, the *Requiem* was born in lies and deceptions. Its creation was powered by the need of money. It was dishonest in its inception, its execution, its manipulation of public opinion, its entire history, and it is still to this day surrounded in controversy.

---

[19] I am certain the women who planned the worldwide event chose Mozart's *Requiem* for its beauty and out of the desire for peace and healing, and that they were not aware of its history and had no inkling of the war that, although already in the works, would not start officially until several months later.

The *Requiem* was commissioned by Austrian nobleman Franz Count von Walsegg, who wanted to pass it off as his own and to claim he had composed it to memorialize the death of his young wife Anna. He wanted to lie to the world. Mozart died having completed only the opening movement, the *Requiem aeternum*, in all of the orchestral and vocal parts. He left a few sequences partially done, completed others only in the vocal parts, and left notes for other sections. Upon his death, his widow Constanze, who was in dire need of money to support herself and her two young sons, wanted to have it completed, in secret, by others so the Count would think Mozart had composed it in its entirety and she could collect the second half of the agreed upon fee. She wanted to lie to the Count, and even asked Süssmayr to forge Mozart's signature. Though it has never been determined with absolute certainty, it is believed that several musicians worked on the *Requiem*, among them, Mozart's students Joseph von Eybler and Freystädtler, as well as his friend Franz Xaver Süssmayr. After it became known that Süssmayr had done most of the work, for the purpose of increasing the impression of authenticity and to be able to receive revenue from its publication and performance, Constanze claimed that Mozart had left explicit instructions for its completion on "little scraps of paper." She wanted to lie to the world and manipulate public opinion. She also had two copies of the *Requiem* made for herself. She sold one to King Friedrich Wilhelm II of Prussia, and the other to publishers Breitkopf & Härtel of Leipzig. In 1799, when the Count learned of the pending publication, he revealed his identity, confessed that he had commissioned it and passed it off as his own, and he asked for a refund of his commission money. At that moment, Süssmayr confessed that he had composed the *Sanctus*, the *Benedictus*, and the *Agnus Dei* in their entirety. Abbé Maximilian Stadler marked the Count's score to indicate which handwriting was Mozart's and which, Süssmayr's. But even knowing this, Breitkopf & Härtel published the first edition as Mozart's work, giving no credit to Süssmayr. They elected to lie to the world. It wasn't until 1826 that André of Offenbach published an edition that recognized Süssmayr's contributions.

Perhaps the most remarkable similarity between the *Requiem* and the American invasions is the fact that both have been left unfinished and that both are collective works. The *Requiem* was not only composed by four or five different musicians in 1791–1792, and sung by thousands of people around the world in 2002, but some scholars believe that they recognize in it the influence of Handel's *Messiah*, of his *Funeral Anthem for Queen Caroline*, and of Pasquale Anfossi's *Sinfonia Venezia*. Some say they also recognize melodic material borrowed from Bach.

Since then, there have been several alternate completions by composers dissatisfied with the traditional "Süssmayr" version. In 1819 Sigismund Neukomm, a student of Joseph Haydn, provided a concluding *Libera me, Domine* for a performance on the feast of St. Cecilia in Rio de Janeiro. Beginning in the 20th Century, we have had completions by several musicologists, including Franz Beyer, Duncan Druce, C. Richard F. Maunder, H.C. Robbins Landon, and Robert D. Levin. Each has attempted to make it more Mozartian by revising the Süssmayr's orchestration, or by using the partial work by Eybler, one of the original contributors, or by dispensing completely with the parts that were written by Süssmayr, but retaining the *Agnus Dei* after discovering an extensive paraphrase from an earlier Mass (Kv.220), or by rewriting entire sections, or by recomposing the ending of the *Lacrimosa* to lead to a complete movement with "Amen" as the text. In 1960, musicologist Wolfgang Plath discovered some sketches for the *Requiem* among Mozart's manuscripts at the Berlin Staatsbibliothek. If these were some of the "scraps of paper" Constanze claimed she had given Süssmayr, then, he also lied. Perhaps in his rush to meet the deadline for the commission, he forgot about the "scraps of paper."[20]

With this brief overview of the history of the *Requiem*, I believe we can safely say that not only did it roll around each time zone of the earth on September [11th] 2002, but also that it has rolled down through the years since the beginning of its composition in 1791. We know who commissioned it and from whom, but we don't know exactly how many versions there are today, or who has played or will play a part in composing or altering each. It is truly an open work of art, in the Umberto Eco sense of *opera aperta*. Ironically, it is a "classical" work that, because it was left unfinished, continues to change, seducing new composers into becoming participants in its completion, which will, however,

---

[20] See *Requiem* (Mozart). *Wikipedia* (Mozart) and Yvonne Grover. "Notes to *Requiem* by Wolfgang Amadeus Mozart: The Robert Levin Completion."

forever remain controversial and unfinished.

And so, Mozart's *Requiem* became for me the most fitting symbol of the American invasions of Iraq and Afghanistan, for their three striking similarities. Both the *Requiem* and the two wars were and continue to be surrounded by lies, secrets, and manipulations. In both cases, we know who started them, but we don't know who will finally and definitively complete them. And, finally, they are not the work of a single individual, family, tribe, social class, political party, or country. They are collaborative works. The collaborations extend across the globe and move backwards and forward in time.

Until recently I believed the first collaborator to be President George Bush the father; I have just learned that he was only the third. The first, according to William Rivers Pitt, was President Jimmy Carter. He says:

> The United States became directly involved with Afghanistan some 38 years ago, on July 3, 1979. On that day, at the behest of National Security Adviser Zhigniew Brzezinski, President Jimmy Carter signed the first directive in an operation meant to destabilize the Soviet-controlled government of Afghanistan. The idea was not to topple that government, but to goad the Soviets into an invasion to protect that government. Brzesinski believed, correctly, that such an occurrence would give the USSR "its Vietnam War."

> [. . . .]

> The Soviets invaded in December of 1979, and over the next 10 years the Reagan administration armed and supported the Mujahadeen "freedom fighters" who later became the Taliban and al-Qaeda. One of the recipients of our largesse in Afghanistan during this time was a wealthy Saudi Arabian ex-pat named Osama bin Laden.

> The Soviets finally retreated in 1989 and crawled home to die. With our geopolitical goals met, the US also withdrew, and Afghanistan collapsed into a blistering civil war, fought with discarded US and Soviet weaponry, that lasted until a Taliban victory in 1996. The country emerged from that

chaos having learned a neat trick: Thanks to the United States, the veterans of these long wars now know how to bring a superpower to its knees. All it takes is time, and patience, and the weapons their enemy left on the battlefield. Not long ago, the US started bombing its own ordnance in Iraq. That's been happening in Afghanistan for decades (Rivers Pitt).

The second collaborator, as Rivers Pitt explains, was Ronald Reagan. During his 8 years as president, the CIA, under Bill Casey, spent billions of dollars to finance, arm, and train the Mujahadeen in Afghanistan to support a jihad against the Soviet Union, which had invaded in 1979. The United States succeeded in driving out the Soviets, but the groups allied to the U.S. gave rise to the Taliban and Osama bin Laden's al-Qaeda.

The third, President George Bush the father, not only bombed Iraq during the Persian Gulf War, and when it was over insisted on extending the sanctions the UN Security Council had originally imposed against Iraq on 6 August 1990, four days after it invaded Kuwait, but by doing so, he set the stage for the revival of American permanent global interventionism. The hawks in his administration celebrated this victory as the end of the "Vietnam-induced malaise," and amid victory parades and celebrations, President George H.W. Bush exclaimed "And, by God, we've kicked the Vietnam syndrome once and for all" (Hartung). This kicking of the Vietnam-induced malaise naturally meant that the United States could go back to its beloved "cover the globe" strategy of responding to any perceived (or invented) foreign threat with planetary military interventions.

The fourth, President Bill Clinton, inherited his initial Iraq policy from his predecessor. Even though the U.S. knew that Iraq had given up its weapons of mass destruction, the Clinton administration insisted on maintaining the sanctions imposed by the United Nations Security Council following Iraq's 1990 invasion of Kuwait. In 1997 he declared, "the sanctions will be there until the end of time or as long as he [Hussein] lasts." Iraq suffered shortages of food, medicines, and clean water. A 1995 *Lancet* study sponsored by the UN Food and Agricultural Organization concluded that 576,000 children under the age of five died because of this policy. Two UN Humanitarian Coordinators in Iraq--Dennis Halliday and Hans von Sponeck--

resigned from the organization to protest what they considered genocide. Jutta Burghardt, the head of the World Food Program, did the same.

One of Clinton's first acts as President was to bomb Baghdad. In 1993 he sent twenty-three cruise missiles to hit the city. Five years later he signed the "Iraq Liberation Act" formalizing the demand for regime change and appropriating $97 million to fund opposition groups. He followed that with Operation Desert Fox, a campaign he sold to the world as retribution for Sadam Hussein's decision to kick UN weapons inspectors out of the country, when in reality it was Clinton who had ordered the inspectors out. Under the guise of enforcing the no-fly zone, the United States, with the help of the United Kingdom, bombed Iraq an average of three times a week from the end of Operation Desert Fox until the 2003 invasion. Chip Gibbons explains that the Clinton policy was part of a bipartisan effort to maintain a continuous war with Iraq in order to keep US hegemony in the Middle East (Gibbons).

The fifth, President George Bush, the son, under the pretense of looking for non-existent weapons of mass destruction, invaded and occupied Iraq with no intention of ever leaving. In his Cheney-Rumsfeld-Wolfowitz-Powell-Rice cabal's dreams of world domination, the plan was to occupy the country, depose its government, write its new constitution, change its economy from state to market, and set up corporate globalization in order to open world markets to U.S. multinationals and maintain U.S. influence in the Middle East and its control over oil, one economy at a time. They wanted to create a "Pax Americana," a new world order that would exceed the dominance over the world exerted by the ancient Roman Empire.

As Tom Engelhardt says:

> At the moment the invasion was launched, in fact, the Pentagon already had plans on the drawing boards for the building of four permanent U.S. mega-bases (initially endearingly labeled "enduring camps") in Iraq on which thousands of U.S. troops could hunker down for an eternity. At the peak of the occupation, there would be more than 500 bases, ranging from tiny combat outposts to ones the size of small American towns--many transformed after 2011 into the ghost towns of a dream gone mad until a few were recently reoccupied by U.S. troops in the battle against the Islamic State (Engelhardt).

The sixth collaborator, President Barack Obama, an early opponent of the war, promised to take the United States off a permanent war footing and was able to fulfill the agreement President Bush had made to withdraw all American troops from Iraq by the end of 2011. Sadly, following the long line of deceptions, that ending was just another lie, for at that point 50,000 troops remained in 94 military bases "advising," "training," "providing security," and carrying out "counter-terrorism missions." As Major General Stephen R. Lanza, the top American military spokesman in Iraq, told *The New York Times,* "in practical terms nothing will change" (Arango). The occupation did not end, it merely changed its mask. As Seumas Milne said, it was simply rebranded (Milne). Rebranded and outsourced. While the number of troops went down, the number of military contractors went up, in an attempt to privatize the war and remain in the occupied country. When the occupation supposedly ended, there were around 100,000 private contractors working for the occupying forces, more than 11,000 of them armed mercenaries, mostly "third country nationals." And the U.S. had plans to increase their numbers. This "surge" of mercenaries was one way to get around the commitment the Bush administration had made to pull all American troops out by the end of 2011.

A second way would have been an Iraqi request for U.S. troops to stay on, and the U.S. tried its best to put together a compliant government that would do so, but in the end, Iraq did not agree to grant impunity from its justice system to American troops that would stay in the country. However, Engelhardt and Tursi say that while the U.S. was negotiating with the Iraqi government, the Pentagon continued to spend hundreds of millions of dollars in military base infrastructure improvements, which it would not have done if it had had any intention of leaving.

A third way was to transfer many of the tasks of the occupation to the State Department and call it "civilian" instead of military. For its enduring presence, the State Department spent around $1.5 billion to set up and run two embassy branch offices and two or more "enduring posts" (a.k.a. "consulates"), employ 2400 people in its Vatican-size embassy in Baghdad, raise the number of private civilian contractors from 2,700 to 7,000, and arm them with castoff Pentagon weaponry and Apache helicopters. The State Department assumed hundreds, perhaps thousands, of other jobs previously handled by the U.S. military (Engelhart and Turse).[21]

Seumas Milne thinks the main reason the United States was so intent on maintaining control of Iraq was the dozen 20-year contracts to run Iraq's oil fields it handed out to foreign corporations, including the three Anglo-American companies that exploited Iraqi oil under British control before the establishment of the Iraqi Republic in 1958, when the Hāshimite monarchy that had been imposed by the British was overthrown. He said in the cited article: "The signs are it [the U.S.] wants to create a new form of outsourced semi-colonial regime to maintain its grip on the country and region."

An example of President Obama's role in the multigenerational deception is the surge in Afghanistan, the 30,000 troops he approved to combat the al-Qaeda "cancer" in that country (in addition to which General Petraeus requested an extra mini-surge of 2000 NATO troops). Obama approved the surge in spite of the fact that his own National Security Adviser, Gen. James Jones, had concluded that there were "fewer than a hundred" al-Qaeda fighters in all of Afghanistan, and in spite of the fact that at a Senate hearing, former Senator John Kerry, D-Mass, asked the CIA Pakistan station chief, Bob Grenier, "So, in terms of Afghanistan, they have been disrupted and dismantled and defeated. They're not in Afghanistan, correct?" and Grenier replied, "That's true" (Esposito, Cole, and Ross).[22] He approved it in spite of the fact that CIA Director Leon Panetta said that there were 50 to 100 al-Qaeda operatives in Afghanistan, maybe less. There were some al-Qaeda in Yemen, and some in Pakistan. There may have been as many as 800 in the three countries combined, while, at the same time, "[a]ccording to Ginger Thompson and Thom Shanker of *The New York Times*, the U.S. military [had] 963 generals and admirals ..." who cost U.S. taxpayers approximately $170 million a year.

While he approved the surge, President Obama also tried to accelerate the withdrawal from Afghanistan. In May 2014, he announced that he was planning to withdraw the last American

---

[21] The authors say that Michael Gordon of *The New York Times* provided most of the numbers they use in their article.

[22] The authors said: "With 100,000 troops in Afghanistan at an estimated yearly cost of $30 billion, it means that for every one al-Qaeda fighter, the U.S. will commit 1,000 troops and $300 million a year."

troops by the end of 2016, leaving only a vestigial force to protect the embassy in Kabul and to help the Afghan military with purchases and other security matters. By August 2015, convinced that the United States would never be able to transform Afghanistan into a democracy able to defend itself, and knowing that there was an emerging terrorist threat that stretched from the Middle East to Africa, he gave up on the idea of nation building and decided that from that moment on America would train and equip foreign armies and leave the front-line fighting to them. He announced that he was halting the withdrawal and leaving thousands of troops in the country, indefinitely. According to Mark Landler, Afghanistan has become "the template for a new kind of warfare — a chronic conflict, across an arc of unstable states, in which the United States is a participant, if not the principal actor" (Landler).

As the seventh collaborator, President Donald Trump threatened the use of nuclear weapons, promised to fill Guantanamo with "bad dudes," designated his first battlefield detainee an enemy combatant, handed the control of the war to "his generals," dropped the "Mother of All Bombs," the most powerful non-nuclear weapon in the Pentagon's arsenal, and tripled the number of bombs that rained on Afghanistan, 3,554 as of 31 October 2017, as compared to 1,337 in all of 2016 and 947 in all of 2015 (Ward).

In his 21 August 2017 remarks at the Fort Myer military base in Arlington, Virginia, on the US military involvement in Afghanistan, he dropped the pretense of "nation building" and admitted that the Afghanistan war is all about hunting and killing "terrorists." But, since 2012, according to the US government, every military-age male in a strike zone is an enemy combatant, which makes nearly all men, including teenagers, "terrorists" (Feroz). In the name of killing terrorists, his generals engaged in the indiscriminate slaughter of innocent people, with women and children being mere collateral damage. As Glenn Greenwald says:

> In other words, Trump has escalated the 16-year-old core premise of America's foreign policy—that it has the right to bomb any country in the world where people it regards as terrorists are found—and in doing so, has fulfilled the warped campaign pledges he repeatedly expressed (Greenwald, "Trump's War...").

Greenwald is correct about the core principle of America's foreign policy, except that this premise is now at least 42 years old, if we begin to count our involvement in Afghanistan on the day when President Jimmy Carter signed the first directive in an operation meant to lure the Soviets into invading Afghanistan. And that is only if we forget about Vietnam and Korea.

Whether we call it Communism or Terrorism, the United States believes that it has the right to bomb any country in the world that stands in the way of natural resources it craves or a geographic position it believes it needs for its full-spectrum dominance.

Now, in 2021, we have in Joseph Robinette Biden, the 46th president of the United States, our eighth and possibly last collaborator. On Wednesday, 14 April 2021, in an address to the nation, he announced that he would end the U.S.'s longest war and withdraw U.S. troops from Afghanistan on the 20th anniversary of the 9/11 terrorist attacks. He said:

> Rather than return to war with the Taliban, we have to focus on the challenges that are in front of us. We have to track and disrupt terrorist networks and operations that spread far beyond Afghanistan since 9/11. We have to shore up American competitiveness to meet the stiff competition we're facing from an increasingly assertive China. We have to strengthen our alliances and work with like-minded partners to ensure that the rules of international norms that govern cyber threats, and emerging technologies that will shape our future are grounded in our democratic values, not those of the autocrats. We have to defeat this pandemic and strengthen the global health system to prepare for the next one, because there will be another pandemic. You know, we'll be much more formidable to our adversaries and competitors over the long term if we fight the battles for the next 20 years, not the last 20 (Biden).

In his remarks, Biden portrayed the war as having begun on 11 September 2001. But, as we know, it was not George W. Bush, but rather Jimmy Carter who was the first collaborator of this war.

After 9/11, Biden voted for the Iraq War. In 2009, as Vice-President, he argued in favor of using the CIA, special operations forces, and drone strikes instead of the large-scale troop surge others favored. This year, as the commander in chief, he said the war was really ending, but with some caveats. The plan that was described is similar to the one he proposed in 2009 as Vice-President. The soldiers in uniform would leave, but he would keep the CIA and special operations teams in the region to use as needed. Administration officials said the U.S. would reposition American troops in the region to keep an eye on Afghanistan and on the Taliban. The troops are not coming home.

In his announcement, Biden said "We were attacked, we went to war with clear goals. We achieved those objectives. Bin Laden is dead and al-Qaeda is degraded in Afghanistan, and it's time to end this forever war." Of course, he did not explain what we did to Afghanistan and to the Soviets starting in 1979. Official history begins when they attack us, not when we provoke the attack.

Biden also said that the United States met its objective ten years ago with the assassination of Taliban leader Osama bin Laden, and since then "Our reasons for staying have become increasingly unclear." In reality, bin Laden had declared war on the United States in 1996, when he issued the first of two *fatwā*s (Arabic: "religious opinions") declaring holy war against the United States, accusing it of looting the natural resources of the Muslim world, the U.S. military presence in Saudi Arabia after the first Gulf War in 1991, and supporting governments submissive to the American interests in the Middle East. Two years later, al-Qaeda bombed the U.S. embassies in Nairobi, Kenya, and Dar es Salaam, Tanzania, killing 224 people. He was also responsible for the 2000 suicide bombing of the USS Cole in the Yemeni port of Aden, where 17 sailors were killed. What Biden does not acknowledge in his announcement is that George W. Bush's administration lied to the world and to the American public because it wanted to wage war on Iraq as the first step of its long-held plans for a *Pax Americana*.

Antonia Juhasz explains that a year before 9/11 the Central Intelligence Agency had warned that the increasing global inequality would

> spawn conflicts at home and abroad, ensuring an even wider gap between regional winners and losers than exists today.... Regions, countries, and groups feeling left behind will face deepening economic stagnation, political instability, and cultural alienation. They will foster political, ethnic, ideological,

and religious extremism, along with the violence that often accompanies it (Juhasz, p. 5).[23]

The Bush administration ignored this warning, and every administration since then has continued to ignore the world-wide conditions of economic stagnation, political instability, and cultural alienation caused by the corporate globalization policy the United States, aided by its three Bretton Woods institutions, has fostered in support of its multinational corporations and their rapacious, violent, and destructive corporate behavior.

The president also said the U.S. would look to reorganize its counterterrorism operations in Afghanistan to help prevent the reemergence of threats to the homeland. That is the truest and most honest part of his remarks. What he proposed was not the end of the war, but a reorganization of the American counterterrorism operations.

Matthew Hoh, a senior fellow at the Center for International Policy, a member of the Eisenhower Media Initiative, and a 100 percent disabled marine combat veteran who resigned his position with the State Department in Afghanistan in 2009 to protest the war said that a genuine peace process in Afghanistan is "dependent upon foreign forces leaving Afghanistan." He added:

> Regardless of whether the 3500 acknowledged U.S. troops leave Afghanistan, the U.S. military will still be present in the form of thousands of special operations and CIA personnel in and around Afghanistan, through dozens of squadrons of manned attack aircraft and drones stationed on land bases and on aircraft carriers in the region, and by hundreds of cruise missiles on ships and submarines (Hoh).

A few days after Biden's announcement, on 20 April, Marine General Frank McKenzie, the top U.S. commander for operations in the Middle East and Central Asia, told House Armed Services Committee members, "Some of the forces are going to remain in Central Command because we are going to look at offshore, over the horizon options." He explained that to conduct counterterror-

---

[23] Global Trends 2015: A Dialogue about the Future with Nongovernment Experts, approved for publication by the National Foreign Intelligence Board under the authority of the Director of Central Intelligence, NIC 2000-02, December 2000 (Juhasz, 363).

ism operations, U.S. forces must be able to do three things: find the target, fix the target, finish the target. He added that an MQ-9 armed drone can be over a target in a "matter of minutes" even if it's based far from Afghanistan. So, with this explanation, we can now understand better what Biden meant by the reorganization of counterterrorism: *offshore* men, "large manned aircraft," and "small unmanned aerial vehicles" to other countries in the region and attack the Taliban and other "bad" actors *over the horizon* with armed drones (Cammarata).

Or, as some current and former American officials said, as reported in the *The New York Times*:

> Instead of declared troops in Afghanistan, the United States will most likely rely on a shadowy combination of clandestine Special Operations forces, Pentagon contractors and covert intelligence operatives to find and attack the most dangerous Qaeda or Islamic State threats (Cooper).

What nobody has spelled out, explained in simple, unambiguous terms, is what counterterrorism means. Counterterrorism, or small footprint antiterrorism, means hunting down and assassinating terrorists, or whoever the United States determines is a threat. This may be done by targeted killings, which are lethal strikes by drones, cruise missiles, and, sometimes, special operations raids. The killings may be conducted by the Department of Defense or, clandestinely, by the CIA. What few understand is that, aside from the moral implications of any extra judicial killing, the targeted or surgical strikes often fail, usually due to faulty information, data gathered by electronic surveillance rather than human intelligence. This results in mistakes that kill a relative of the intended victim, a group of strangers, or an entire wedding party.

Because Biden said in his remarks of 14 April that he will keep the CIA and special operations teams in the region to use as needed, it appears that the longest U.S. war is not really ending. Once more, it is merely being rebranded, and from now on, it will rely exclusively on "a shadowy combination of clandestine Special Operations forces, Pentagon contractors and covert intelligence operatives" (Cooper).

When Biden introduced his nominees for top national security positions at the Queen Theater in Wilmington, Delaware, on 24 November 2020, he said they will "restore America globally, its global leadership and its moral leadership." As part of restoring

America's moral leadership, the nominees spoke of championing human rights and improving multilateral relationships with allies and democracies around the world. His national security adviser, Jake Sullivan, said, Mr. President-elect:

> You have also tasked us with putting people at the center of our foreign policy. You have told us the alliances we rebuild, the institutions we lead, the agreements we sign, all of them should be judged by a basic question—will this make life better, easier, safer for families across this country? (Wilkie).

While it is true that at least half of Americans are happy for the efforts President Biden is making, in spite of the opposition from Republicans, to solve the most urgent problems he inherited from his predecessor, I want to believe that moral leadership should not be limited to the internal problems of the United States, but should instead extend to all the peoples of the Earth. And to continue to give verbal, diplomatic, military, and financial support ($3.8 billion in annual grants from the U.S. government) to Israel, whose only goal is to construct a "Greater Israel" by terrorizing and pushing Palestinians out of their land is the farthest thing from exercising moral leadership any person or government could possibly claim.

The sale of advanced military technology to Saudi Arabia is still pending while the administration conducts a review to determine which weapons can be used for offensive purposes and which can be construed to have a self-defense purpose. The review emphasizes the hypocrisy of this and all previous administrations, for we know that the U.S. wants to sell as many armaments to as many countries as possible, for weapons is one of the few products this country, whose main industry is making war, manufactures anymore.

Sadly, the Biden administration is not selling weapons only to Saudi Arabia, the United Arab Emirates, and Israel. In the months he has been in power, the man who ran his campaign on the promise to end forever wars and to base his foreign policy on human rights and racial justice has sold weapons to at least 3 governments that are human rights abusers. In February, it approved plans to sell Egypt missiles worth $197 million. In addition to the missiles, Egypt receives $1.3 billion in annual security assistance from the U.S. In May, it approved a sale of precision-guided weapons to Israel for $735 million. That same month, Israeli strikes killed 260 Palestinians in Gaza, at least 129 of them civilians, including 66 children. In June, the administration notified Congress of a proposed sale of more than $2.5 billion in arms to the Philippines, including fighter jets and 2 kinds of precision missiles, even though the International Criminal Court has accused the government of President Rodrigo Duterte of crimes against humanity (Epstein).

Even though armaments have become one of the few growth industries we have left, one of our few sources of jobs, we must not forget what President Dwight D. Eisenhower said in his *Cross of Iron* speech: "Every gun that is made, every warship launched, every rocket fired signifies, in the final sense, a theft from those who hunger and are not fed, those who are cold and are not clothed." President Eisenhower said this on 16 April 1953. The country did not listen, and 14 years later, almost to the day, on 4 April 1967, Reverend Martin Luther King delivered his *Beyond Vietnam* sermon in Riverside Church. The country again did not listen, and we are suffering the results of that willful refusal to hear. Eisenhower added in his speech, "This world in arms is not spending money alone. It is spending the sweat of its laborers, the genius of its scientists, the hopes of its children." Following his line of thinking, I can only say that when laborers work building machines of death, their souls deaden themselves. When scientists utilize their imagination to create instruments of death, their souls atrophy. When children live in a violent, materialistic, society, when they are deprived of food, medical care, schooling, a safe environment, a loving family, their dreams wilt in their souls.

Biden has said again and again that he wants to improve the lives of Americans. To continue bombing, invading, and occupying other countries in the pursuit of world primacy does the opposite. To continue supporting morally, diplomatically, financially, and with armaments countries that commit crimes against humanity does the opposite of improving the lives of Americans. By selling armaments and providing financial support to Egypt, the Philippines, and Israel, he is giving his approval for murdering human beings, most of whom are probably innocent victims of abusive would-be dictators. If Jeremy Scahill is correct and Joe Biden is "a man who is dedicated to the U.S. as an empire, who believes that preserving U.S. national interests and 'prestige' on the global stage outweighs considerations of morality or even at times the deaths of innocent people" (Scahill, *Video*), then he will not be able to save the soul of America. An Empire is never a principled entity. It is a history of crimes, transactional relations, and the selling of its soul one lie at a time, one deal at a time, one bullet at a time.

In the "Beyond Vietnam" sermon he delivered in Riverside Church in New York City, on 4 April 1967, Dr. Martin Luther King warned that "a nation that continues year after year to spend more money on military defense than on programs of social uplift is approaching spiritual death."

> As I have walked among the desperate, rejected, and angry young men, I have told them that Molotov cocktails and rifles would not solve their problems... But they asked, and rightly so, "what about Vietnam?" They asked if our own nation wasn't using massive doses of violence to solve its problems, to bring about the changes it wanted. Their questions hit home, and I knew that I could never again raise my voice against the violence of the oppressed in the ghettos without having first spoken clearly to the greatest purveyor of violence in the world today: my own government.

If Dr. King were delivering his speech today, the desperate, rejected, and angry young people he would be trying to help would ask him "what about Chile? what about Haiti? what about Nicaragua? what about Cuba, Puerto Rico, Mexico, Guatemala, Colombia, Panama, El Salvador, Honduras, Dominican Republic, Grenada, Venezuela? What about Iraq and Afghanistan? What about 191 countries of the world?" Since 1776, the United States has been at war 226 out of 244 years. It has been militarily involved with 191 out of 193 countries, or 98% of the world, with some, more than once. Despite closing hundreds of bases in Iraq and Afghanistan, it still maintains almost 1000 in more than 80 countries and territories abroad.

As Dr. King said in his speech, Vietnam was only a symptom of a deeper malady in the American spirit. That spiritual illness has only gotten worse since that day.

President Biden campaigned and is governing guided by the claim that he wants to restore the soul of America. I don't know whether he is familiar with King's "Beyond Vietnam" speech or with the fact that in 1957, when King and other civil rights activists formed the Southern Christian Leadership Conference, they chose as their motto: "To save the soul of America." I would like to ask President Biden to make an adjustment to his motto. I believe King's "save the soul" is a better term because you cannot restore what was never there.

What is the soul of this country? Sadly, up to now, the soul of the United States has been held hostage to its desire to be the indispensable nation, the one entitled to rule and exploit all the others, and for that goal, it has backed dictators, orchestrated coups and murders of foreign leaders, attacked nations fighting for independence, tortured and trained torturers, built an arsenal of nuclear weapons and exploded the only 2 that have been detonated to date. It built a military larger than the next 10 or 12 countries combined, is number 1 in global arms sales, supports a racist, militarized police force in almost every city and county in the country, has a great concentration of wealth in the hands of a tiny oligarchic minority and vast areas of shameful, inhumane, poverty and neglect in the rest of the population. It is the only developed country without a universal health care system, an adequate social safety net, or a civilized, forward-looking system of laws that care for families, one that puts the human at the center of society. Can it honestly claim to have even an embryonic *soul*?

Can we as individuals or as a nation ignore or contribute to the suffering of others, whether inside or outside our borders, and still save our soul? Can we claim to be the indispensable nation and to personify moral leadership on this earth while continuing to support the abuses, the cruelty, the racism of Israel? Can we continue to deny the damage we have caused in Iraq and Afghanistan in pursuit of primacy? Can we continue to ignore the attempts of White Supremacists to disenfranchise Blacks and other minorities? Can we give them a pass for their attacks on our Constitution and their violence against anybody and anything they consider "other"? Can we pretend we don't see the lack of equity and justice within our own borders? Can we be blind to the physical and spiritual suffering of our poor, our homeless, our hungry, our addicted, our sick and lonely masses? Can we keep saying we don't have enough money for them while continuing to spend billions on weapons systems we don't need because nobody is attacking us?

As King said, America, the richest and most powerful nation in the world can well lead the way in the radical revolution of values the world needs. "When machines and computers, profit motives and property rights, are considered more important than people, the giant triplets of racism, extreme materialism, and militarism are incapable of being conquered" (*Beyond Vietnam*).

On 27 June 2021, Washington launched its third airstrike against Iraq and Syria, two countries illegally occupied by the US military, which have repeatedly called for American troops to leave. In December 2019, the Trump administration bombed anti-ISIS militias in both countries. Biden carried out a similar attack in eastern Syria in February 2021. The December 2019, February 2021, and June 2021 airstrikes targeted the Iraqi government-backed Popular Mobilization Forces known in Arabic as the al-Hashd al-Sha'abi. In its official statement on the June bombing, the Pentagon stated that it was attacking Kata'ib Hezbollah and Kata'ib Sayyid al-Shuhada, two Iraqi armed groups in the Hashd. The Pentagon tried to justify its attack claiming it was an act of "self-defense." Under international law, a military that is illegally occupying a territory does not have the right to self-defense. Iraq's prime minister, Mustafa al-Kadhimi condemned the strikes as an "unacceptable violation of Iraqi sovereignty and Iraqi national security" (El Khoury).

In January 2020, in response to Washington's assassination of Iranian General Qasem Soleimani and Iraqi Commander Abu Mahdi al-Muhan, the Iraqi parliament voted unanimously to expel the thousands of US troops occupying Iraq. Washington ignored the vote, and threatened more economic sanctions. The U.S. is also illegally occupying one-third of Syria. The government in Damascus has repeatedly called on the US military to leave, but it has refused, in violation of Syrian sovereignty. Glenn Greenwald says:

> Indeed, anyone invested in endless war in the Middle East —
> including the entire U.S. intelligence community and the
> weapons industry which feeds off of it — must be thrilled by
> all of this. Each time the U.S. "retaliates" against Iran or
> Iraqi militias or Syrian fighters, it causes them to "retaliate"
> back, which in turn is cited as the reason the U.S. can never
> leave but must instead keep retaliating, ensuring this cycle
> never ends. It also creates a never-ending supply of angry
> people in that region who hate the U.S. for bringing death
> and destruction to their countries with bombs that never
> stop falling and therefore want to strike back: what we are all
> supposed to call "terrorism." That is what endless war means:
> a war that is *designed* never to terminate, one that is as far
> removed as possible from actual matters of self-defense and
> manufactures its own internal rationale to continue it
> (Greenwald).

On 30 June 2021, 113 anti-war, human rights, environmental, and religious rights organizations from across the world wrote to President Biden to demand an end to airstrikes, including drone attacks, outside any recognized battlefield. The letter reminds Biden of his promise to end forever wars and to base his foreign policy on human rights. The signatories say that "disavowing and ending the lethal strikes program is both a human rights and racial justice imperative in meeting these commitments" (People's Dispatch). As Martin Luther King said: "A nation that continues year after year to spend more money on military defense than on programs of social uplift is approaching spiritual death."

Many people said that there was no real grand design to the war in Afghanistan, that its only purpose was to continue asking Congress for multi-billion dollar budgets that would be funneled to private contractors (Ludwig). They were partially correct. Enriching private contractors was one of the key purposes of the wars in Iraq and Afghanistan, and, later, of the wars in the Greater Middle East and parts of Africa.

A second purpose was, as both William Rivers Pitt and Kevin Zeese pointed out, to take possession of the oil in Iraq and the rich mineral resources that the U.S. Geological Survey discovered lying under Afghanistan's soil: rare earth minerals needed for high tech, energy, and industrial applications; rich deposits of precious gems; and, of course, also the bumper poppy crops that Afghanistan has enjoyed since it was invaded in 2001 (Rivers Pitt). A 2017 CNBC report explained that according to a partial survey by the Afghan Ministry of Mines and Petroleum, the country's mineral wealth is estimated to be at least $3 trillion.

The third purpose of invading Afghanistan and the other countries in the Greater Middle East was geopolitical. According to Kevin Zeese:

> Just as the United States has stayed in Germany, Italy and other European states and Japan after WWII, and in Korea after the Korean war, the empire sees a need to be in Afghanistan to be well positioned for the future of the empire. Terrorism is not the issue, economic competition with China, which is quickly becoming the leading global economic power, is the real issue.

And, competition with Russia and China is at the top of the list of the bi-partisan war party in Washington.

Pepe Escobar says:

> So from the point of view of neocon/neoliberalcon elements of the War Party in Washington, Afghanistan only makes sense as a forward base to harass/stall/thwart China's Belt and road Initiative.

Congresswoman Barbara Lee of Oakland, who on 14 September 2001 cast the only vote against the Authorization for Use of Military Force that preceded the military action against Afghanistan saying, "Let us not become the evil we deplore," is now leading a group of fifty House members who sent a letter to President Biden urging him to slash the Pentagon budget. In their letter, they said:

> Hundreds of billions of dollars now directed to the military would have greater return if invested in diplomacy, humanitarian aid, global public health, sustainability initiatives, and basic research. We must end the forever wars, heal our veterans, and re-orient towards a holistic conception of national security that centers public health, climate change and human rights (Kheel).

Going back to the collaborators of the lies, secrets, and manipulations of the two wars, in addition to the eight presidents, we must mention the coalition of 43 countries, including all the members of NATO, and other compliant allies who have participated in one or more of the American attacks and invasions of Iraq and Afghanistan.

Despite having proven ourselves incapable of permanently pacifying and rebuilding any of the countries we have invaded in the last 20 years, and under the cloak of different euphemisms—"advising," "training," "providing security," "partnering," etc., the American military continues to occupy Iraq, and on 30 August 2021, just a few hours before the deadline the Taliban had promised to enforce, abandoned Afghanistan in an embarrasingly rushed, chaotic, and bloody exit.

The energy we have spent bombing, invading, torturing, and destroying has resulted in an increase of entropy across the Earth and here at home. We are suffering from an economic crisis, a pandemic, the militarization of the policing of urban America, with its humiliation and dehumanization of "the enemy," in this case our own minority populations, in what is dangerously resembling the "occupied territory" of our imperial counterinsurgencies, *e.g.* St. Louis cops chanting "Whose streets? *Our* streets," after making arrests of protesters on 18 September 2017. As Danny Sjursen says: "American society is embracing its inner empire" (Sjursen). We are also under the attack on the rule of law and the U.S. Constitution, a violent attempted coup of the U.S. Capitol, an on-going assault on democracy itself by the Republican Party passing ever-more expansive rules designed to sabotage the electoral process and disenfranchise the poor and racial minorities.

We are experiencing an epidemic of diseases of despair. These soul illnesses include alcoholism, gambling, depression, morbid obesity, opioid addictions, incest, rape, sexual obsession, femicides, suicides, intra-family murders, and mass shootings, almost daily mass shootings. The Empire has come home. We have become our own "others," the humiliated, dehumanized, and often dead collateral damage the Empire leaves in its wake.

Or, as Samuel Taylor Coleridge would suggest, like the Ancient Mariner, we have hung the carcass of the Albatross we murdered around our own necks.

I began preparing myself mentally for the writing of the poems included in this collection while watching the events of September 11th 2002, for on that day, together with pride and sadness, I felt apprehension about the rumors that the United States was already preparing to attack Iraq.[24] I was suffused with a sense of irony. I felt that any desire for revenge was a betrayal of my mourning and

---

[24] This collection includes poems about President George H. W. Bush's Persian Gulf War, about the years of his sanctions, about the Sadam Hussein dictatorship, and, mostly, about President George W. Bush's invasion and occupation of Iraq and Afghanistan. In my long bilingual poem, *Lengua lanzadera enhebrada / Tongue Threaded Shuttle.* Sonora: Editorial Garabatos, 2017, I have sections about the Bush family, the American Empire, and other empires throughout history.

of the grief most humans were experiencing that day. An attack would be a violation of the solidarity expressed in every language, in every corner of the world, a disloyalty to the desire many of the most affected had expressed for peace and forgiveness, a desertion of Reverend Lyndon Harris's 260-day season of renewal "in which people of love and goodwill, compassion and generosity, sought to practice the art of radical hospitality" and through their "reciprocity of gratitude" tried to "reclaim humanity from the violence that sought to make human life less human" ("Sanctuary").

I felt it would be ironic to use this great human tragedy as an excuse for waging war against a country that had played no role in the previous year's attack on the United States, a country everybody knew was a target for its oil reserves. And if the planning of the invasion, its execution, the twenty years of official occupation, the millions of people, Afghans, Iraqis, and invaders, killed, maimed, tortured, imprisoned, disappeared, impoverished, made homeless, mentally deranged, or spiritually dehumanized, and the misuse of American treasure that has bankrupted this country and hurt the entire world were not enough, we now have a "longest war" that has ended, but with caveats. At a minimum, the United States is reserving for itself the right to continue "over the horizon" illegal drone strikes, even if that means murdering 10 members of an innocent civilian family.

I didn't know all this on 11 September 2002, but I had a premonition. I sensed it was a tragi-comic irony of cosmic proportions designed by a bunch of charlatans with a god complex, carried out by the one percent of the population that, mostly poor and undereducated, has military service in its D.N.A., and approved by the rest of us who, too busy and too selfish to pay attention to what the politicians we elect to serve us are doing to fill their pockets and salve their egos, have fallen for "Support our troops," the mantra that has robbed us of our ability to think and question.

William J. Astore, a retired lieutenant colonel (USAF) who has a Doctor of Philosophy degree in modern history from the University of Oxford, and who has taught at the Air Force Academy, the Naval Postgraduate School, and the Pennsylvania College of Technology, has written an article explaining the reasons why the United States cannot stop making war. He says we wage war because we're good at it. We believe we have the best trained troops, the most advanced weapons, and the purest motives. We see ourselves as "freedom-bringers" rather than as "death-dealers" and resource exploiters. We have come to dominate the global arms trade, and "endless war" has become "endlessly profitable" for defense corporations and private contractors and for the senators and representatives they lobby. With the use of high technology drones and predators armed with Hellfire missiles, the casualties of American sons and daughters have been limited. This emotional distancing of the true cost of war has been increased with the use of private military contractors. Death has become something that happens to others in far away lands (Astore).

As fear of poverty drove Constanze Mozart into lying and manipulation, so fear has driven us, Americans, into allowing the State propaganda machine to convince us that bad people, Muslims, undocumented border crossers, and terrorists lurking everywhere, especially inside brown skins, are at our doors and ready to destroy us. Driven by this fear, we have allowed our entire society to become militarized. Our media, embedded with the powers that be at home as well as in the battlefield, our intelligence agencies, our foreign policy gurus, our "homeland security" apparatus, including our border patrol and the national guard troops on our southern border, are all intertwined with military priorities, and with the politicians who profit from a society organized around military agendas.

In this militarized society, any heart-felt criticism of our wars is considered un-American. Driven by fear and laziness, we have all become participants in this Imperial Enterprise. Allowing fear of terrorism, of economic hardship, of legal reprisals, including imprisonment, should we be branded as "un-American," we cave in and join the hordes calling for racial hatreds and religious crusades. Giving in to intellectual laziness, we buy the propaganda that keeps us from finding out the truth about American history and American government and accepting the State's lies and deceptions. Signing on to the myths and the brainwashing we grew up with, we continue deceiving ourselves into believing in our own goodness and generosity, in our being the beacon of liberty and democracy for the entire world. We want to continue believing, and our politicians remind us, that we are the indispensable nation and that our destiny gives us the right to feel superior, to ignore the dozens of countries we have destroyed and the millions of people we have bombed, tortured, incinerated, in order to be able to support our "American Way of Life."

Were we to face our anesthetized conscience, we would have to admit that our collaboration did not begin on 9/11. We would have to remember the Gulf War, Vietnam, Hiroshima, Nagasaki, all the business deals our leaders made with the Nazis, Korea, the Spanish-American War, the Mexican-American War, the civil wars and invasions we promoted in Latin America, "our back yard," and the petty dictators we imposed on them, the American Indian Genocide, and thousands of other overt and covert murderous activities in every corner of the globe. Were we ever to face ourselves with absolute honesty, we would be horrified by what we have become, and we would be obliged to convene Mozart and his collaborators, past and future, and ask them to set up an academy to compose hundreds, thousands, perhaps millions, of requiems, masses for the dead sung in many tongues to promise *lux aeterna* to all the brown-skinned peoples of the earth the Empire chooses to assassinate.

We would also have to ask them to compose another type of mass. A mass for a dead conscience, for the conscience of a society that calls itself a civilization and is proud to train its young as consummate murderers, to have as its principal industry the manufacture of ever-more advanced and destructive weapons systems, to indoctrinate its people with feelings of self-importance, an attitude of entitlement, a complete disregard for the suffering of others. A society that has "In God We Trust" on its currency, and uses this currency, this economic might, to build the largest arsenal the world has ever known and to feel entitled to control and dominate, to annihilate, if necessary, the rest of humanity. A society determined to ravage the Earth. A society that ignores the health of mothers and babies, the education of children, the well-being of young families, the lives of military-age men and women, the respect of elders. A society that neglects the maintenance of its infrastructure, the economic future of its citizens, the ethics of its public servants, the nurturing of its talent, the blossoming of culture and the arts. A society that admires wealth and despises the poor. A society that respects raw power and shows contempt for spiritual clarity. A civilization, not of life, but of Death.

Tucson, Arizona, 11 September 2002—
Philadelphia, Pennsylvania, 30 December 2021

Works Consulted

Aikins, Matthieu. Interview by Amy Goodman and Juan González. "U.S. Drone Killed 10 Afghans, Including Aid Worker and 7 Kids, After Water Jugs Were Mistaken as Bombs." *Democracy Now!,* democracynow.org, *The War and Peace Report,* 15 Sept. 2021. Web.

Aikins, Matthieu, Christoph Koetti, Evan Hill and Eric Schmitt. "Times Investigation: In U.S. Drone Strike, Evidence Suggests No ISIS Bomb." *New York Times* 10 Sept. 2021. Updated 15 Sept. 2021. Web.

Amini, Mariam. "At stake in US military efforts to stabilize Afghanistan: At least $3 trillion in natural resources." *CNBC,* 19 Aug. 2017, updated 21 Aug. 2017. Web.

Amiry, Sharif. "Taliban Threatens US With Countermeasures: Taliban Backs Out of Planned Talks As US Extends Troop Presence." *TOLO News TV Network,* 15 Apr. 2021. Web.

Andelman, David A. "France says Australian Submarine deal with U.S. is a slap in the face. And it is." *Think, NBC News,* 17 Sept. 2021. Web.

Arango, Tim. "War in Iraq Defies U.S. Timetable for End of Combat." *New York Times,* 2 July 2010. Web.

Astore, William J. "Hope and Change Fade, but War Endures: Seven Reasons Why We Can't Stop Making War." *TomDispatch.com,* 8 July 2010. Web.

---. "The pentagon as pentagod: America's abyss of weapons and warmaking." *TomDispatch,* 16 November, 2021. Web.

Bacevich, Andrew J. "Prepare, Pursue, Prevail: Onward and Upward with U.S. Central Command." *TomDispatch.com,* 21 Mar.2017. Web.

Bacevich, Andrew J. and Annelle Sheline. "The End of American Militarism?" Biden Must Confront Washington's Addiction to Force." *Foreign Affairs*, 15 Oct. 2021. Web.

Balfour, Arthur James. "Balfour Declaration." *Wikipedia*, 2 Nov. 1917. Web.

Biden, Joseph. "Remarks by President Biden on the Way Forward in Afghanistan." *White House Speeches and Remarks*, 14 Apr. 2021. Web.

---. "Readout of President Joseph R. Biden, Jr. Meeting with Prime Minister Al-Kadhimi of Iraq." *White House Statements and Releases*, 26 July, 2021. Web.

---. "Remarks by President Biden Before the 76th Session of the United Nations General Assembly." United Nations Headquarters, New York, New York. *White House Speeches and Remarks*, 21 Sept. 2021. Web.

Billing, Lynzy. "The U.S. Is Leaving Afghanistan? Tell That to the Contractors. American firms capitalize on the withdrawal, moving in with hundreds of new jobs." *Intelligencer,* 12 May 2021. Web.

Brands, Hal and John Lewis Gaddis. "The New Cold War: America, China, and the Echoes of History." *Foreign Affairs*, Nov./Dec. 2021. Web.

Brown, Gordon. "on the need for a new multeralism." *The Economist*, 17 Sept. 2021. Web.

Cammarata, Sarah. "Centcom general warns fighting terrorism will become difficult once US troops leave Afghanistan." *Stars and Stripes,* 20 Apr. 2021. Web.

Chomsky, Noam. "on the cruelty of American imperialism." *The Economist*, 24 Sept. 2021. Web.

Chomsky, Noam. Interview by C. J. Polychroniou. "Without US Aid, Israel Wouldn't Be Killing Palestinians En Masse." *Truthout,* 12 May 2021. Web.

Cohen, Roger and Michael D. Shear. "Furious Over Sub Deal, France Recalls Ambassadors to U.S. and Australia." *New York Times*, 17 Sept. 2021. Updated 18 Sept. 2021. Web.

Cohn, Marjorie. "War in Afghanistan Isn't Over--It's Taking the Form of Illegal Drone Strikes." *Truthout*, 26 Sept. 2021. Web.

Cooper, Helen, Thomas Gibbons-Neff, and Eric Schmitt. "Biden to Withdraw All Combat Troops From Afghanistan by Sept. 11." *New York Times,* 13 April, updated 24 July, 2021. Web.

Editorial Board. "The Pentagon Is Not a Sacred Cow." *New York Times*, 13 Dec. 2017. Web.

Editorial Board. "Who Abandoned Bagram Air Base? Biden says the military, but the military says he gave them little choice." *Wall Street Journal*, 27 Aug. 2021. Web.

Eisenhower, Dwight D. "Cross of Iron" speech. Delivered to the American Society of Newspaper Editors at the Statler Hotel, Washington, D.C. on 16 April 1953. *American Rhetoric Online Speech Bank.* Web.

El Khoury, Bachir with Laura El Khoury. "Pro-Iran Militias Attack US Base in Syria After Air Strikes." *International Business Times,* 28 June 2021. Web.

Emmons, Alex, and Nick Turse. "Biden's War Policy Offers Chance For Change--Or More of the Same." *Intercept,* 7 Mar. 2021. Web.

Encyclopaedia Britannica. Web.

Engelhardt, Tom. "Bombs Away! Their Precision Weaponry and Ours." *TomDispatch.com,* 8 Sept. 2016. Web.

---. "President Blowback: How the Invasion of Iraq Came Home." *TomDispatch.com*, 16 Mar. 2017. Web.

---. "Whose Century Is It? Life on an Increasingly Improbable Planet." *TomDispatch.com,* 7 July 2016. Web.

Engelhardt, Tom and Nick Turse. "The American Way of War Quiz: This Was the War Month That Was (Believe It or Not)" *TomDispatch.com*, 14 Sept. 2010. Web.

Epstein, Elisa. "It's time for the U.S. to stop selling weapons to human rights abusers." *Washington Post*, 21 July 2021. Web.

Escobar, Pepe. "Korea, Afghanistan and the Never Ending War Trap." *Asia Times*, 23 Aug. 2017, Web.

Esposito, Richard, Matthew Cole and Brian Ross. "President Obama's Secret: Only 100 al Qaeda Now in Afghanistan." *ABC News, The Blotter*, 2 Dec. 2009. Web.

Ferguson, Niall. "on why the end of America's empire won't be peaceful." *The Economist*, 20 Aug. 2021. Web.

Feroz, Emran. "The U.S. Bombed Afghanistan More in September Than Any Month Since 2010, But the Toll Remains Hidden." *In These Times*, 16 Oct. 2017. Web.

Fukuyama, Francis. "on the end of American hegemony." *The Economist*, 18 Aug. 2021. Web.

George, Susannah. "Afghanistan's military collapse: Illicit deals and mass desertion." *Washington Post*, 15 Aug. 2021. Web.

George, Susannah, Missy Ryan, Tyler Pager, Pamela Constable, John Hudson and Griff Witte. "Surprise, panic and fateful choices: The day America lost its longest war." *Washington Post*, 28 Aug. 2021. Web.

Ghosh, Amitav. *The Nutmeg's Curse: Parables for a Planet in Crisis*. Chicago: The University of Chicago Press, 2021. Web.

Gibbons, Chip. "When Iraq Was Clinton's War." *Jacobin Magazine*, 6 May 2016. Web.

Giroux, Henry A. "Jim Crow Politics Have Descended on Education." *Truthout*, 27 Oct. 2021. Web.

---. "Three Fundamentalisms Are Driving the Resurgence of Fascist Politics in the U.S." *Truthout*, 1 April, 2021. Web.

Green, Elliott A. "The Curious Careers of Two Advocates of Arab Nationalism." *Crossroads* No. 33, 1992. Web.

Greenberg, Karen J. "'Enemy Combatants' Again? Will Washington Never Learn?" *TomDispatch.com*, 15 Oct. 2017. Web.

Greenwald, Glenn. "Biden's Bombing of Iraq and Syria Only Serves the Weapons Industry."*Popular Resistance.org*, 29 June 2021. Web.

---. "Trump's War on Terror Has Quickly Become as Barbaric and Savage as He Promised." *Intercept*, 26 Mar. 2017. Web.

Grover, Yvonne. "Notes to *Requiem* by Wolfgang Amadeus Mozart: The Robert Levin Completion." *Wikipedia* (Mozart). Web.

Haass, Richard N. "How a World Order Ends: And What Comes in the Wake." *Foreign Affairs*, 98 No. 1 2019, 22-30. Web.

---. "The Age of American First: Washington's Flawed New Foreign Policy Consensus." *Foreign Affairs*, Nov./Dec. 2021. Web.

Hartung, William D. "The Urge to Splurge." *TomDispatch.com*, 25 Oct. 2016. Web.Hedges, Chris. "On American Sadism." *ScheerPost.com*. 4 July 2021. Web.

Heer, Jeet. "The CIA Is Running Death Squads in Afghanistan." *Nation*, 21 Dec. 2020. Web.

Hoh, Matthew. "The U.S. Government Will Not Withdraw Forces from Afghanistan." *Institute for Public Accuracy*, 14 Apr. 2021. Web.

Hussain, Murtaza. "Joe Biden Promises a Moral Renewal for the U.S. Here's Where He Can Start." *Intercept*, 2 Sept. 2020. Web.

Immerwahr, Daniel. "How the US has hidden its empire." *The Guardian.com,* 15 Feb. 2019. Web.

Juhasz, Antonia. *The Bush Agenda: Invading the World, One Economy at a Time.* Harper-Collins e-books, 6 Oct. 2009. William Morrow, First Edition, 25 April 2006.

---. Interview by Joshua Holland. "Bush Clears the Way for Corporate Domination." *Alternet,* 5 May 2006. Web.

King, Martin Luther, Jr. "Beyond Vietnam—A Time to Break Silence." Delivered 4 Apr. 1967 in Riverside Church, New York City. *American Rhetoric Online Speech Bank.* Web.

King-Crane Commission Report. Section under "Zionism," 28 Aug. 1919. Web.

Knox, Oliver with research by Caroline Anders. "Biden could soon end the Iraq War (no, really). *The Daily, Washington Post,* 30 November 2021. Web.

Krugman, Paul. "Errors and Lies." *New York Times,* 18 May 2015. Web.

---. "The Biggest Tax Scam in History." *New York Times,* 27 Nov. 2017. Web.

---. "The Republican War on Children." *New York Times,* 7 Dec. 2017. Web.

Landler, Mark. "The Afghan War and the Evolution of Obama." *New York Times,* 1 Jan. 2017. Web.

List of papal bulls. *Wikipedia,* the free encyclopedia. Web

Lobe, Jim. "Pentagon Moving Swiftly to Become 'GloboCop." *Inter Press Service,* 10 June, 2003. Web.

Ludwig, Mike. "The Hard Numbers on the War in Afghanistan Trump Left Out of His Speech." *Popularresistance.org,* 23 Aug. 2017. Web.

Mathis, Joel. "Biden won't reconsider America's imperial reach." *The Week*, 30 November 2021. Web.

McConnell, David A. "A Guide to Mozart: Requiem." *The Classic Review*, 27 May 2020. Web.

McCoy, Alfred W. *To Govern the Globe: World Orders and Catastrophic Change*. Chicago: Haymarket Books,2021. Web.

McKinley, P. Michael. "We All Lost Afghanistan: Two Decades of Mistakes, Misjudgments, and Collective Failure." *Foreign Affairs*, 16 Aug. 2021. Web.

Mearsheimer, John J. "The Inevitable Rivalry: America, China, and the Tragedy of Great-Power Politics." *Foreign Affairs*, Nov./Dec. 2021. Web.

Miliband, David. "The Age of Impunity and How to Fight It." *Foreign Affairs,* 13 May 2021. Web.

Milne, Seumas. "The US Isn't Leaving Iraq, It's Rebranding the Occupation." *The Guardian*, 5 Aug. 2010. Rpt. in *World News Daily Information Clearing House,* 5 Aug. 2010. Web.

Neimark, Benjamin, Oliver Belcher, and Patrick Bigger. "US military is a bigger polluter than as many as 140 countries—shrinking this war machine is a must." *Conversation,* 24 June 2019. Web.

Norton, Ben. "US bombing of Iraq and Syria is illegal aggression--Occupiers have no right to 'self-defense'." *Al Mayadeen.net,* 29 June 2021. Web.

Nye, Joseph. "The new Rome meets the new barbarians." *The Economist*, 23 Mar 2002. Web.

Obama, Barack. "Remarks by the President at the National Defense University." The White House, Office of the Press Secretary, 23 May 2013. Web.

---. "Remarks by the President in Address to the Nation on Syria." The White House, Office of the Press Secretary, 10 Sept. 2013. Web.

People's Dispatch. "Groups Demand End to 'Unlawful' US Airstrikes and Drone Attacks." *Popular Resistance.org.,* 5 July 2021. Web.

Petersen-Smith, Khury. "Saudi Arabia Arms Sale Is One of Biden's Many Militaristic Actions in First Year." *Truthout,* 12 Dec. 2021. Web.

Philipps, Dave. "U.S. Troops Are Still Deploying to Iraq, Even as Afghan War Ends." *New York Times,* 29 Sept. 2021. Web.

Quilty, Andrew. "The CIA's Afghan Death Squads." *Intercept,* 18 Dec. 2020. Web.

Rao, Nirupama. "on America's need for wisdom and allies in Asia." *The Economist,* 27 Sept. 2021. Web.

Rivers Pitt, William. "Afghanistan War Year 38: Trump Wants More." *Truthout,* 24 Aug. 2017. Web.

---. "Biden Tried to Absolve Himself for Afghanistan Aftermath—But He Voted for War." *Truthout,* 20 July 2021. Web.

Roy, Arundhati. "on America's fiery, brutal impotence." *The Economist,* 3 Sept. 2021. Web.

Rubin, Jennifer. "Opinion: Defense officials just debunked much of the criticism of Biden's Afghanistan withdrawal." *Washington Post,* 28 Sept. 2021. Web.

St. Clair, Jeffrey. "The War That Time Forgot." *Counterpunch.org,* 25 Aug. 2017. Web.

"Sanctuary at Ground Zero." *National Geographic Magazine,* Sept. 2002. Web.

Scahill, Jeremy. "Empire Politician: A Half-Century of Joe Biden's Stances on War, Militarism, and the CIA." *Intercept*, 18 Dec. 2020. Web.

Scahill, Jeremy. Interview by Amy Goodman and Juan González. Part 1: "Empire Politician: Joe Biden's Half-Century Record on Foreign Policy, War, Militarism & the CIA." *Democracy Now!* democracynow.org, 28 Apr. 2021. Web.

Part 2: Jeremy Scahill: "Joe Biden's Foreign Policy Record Shows Evolution of U.S. Empire Since Vietnam War." *Democracy Now!* democracynow.org, 28 Apr. 2021. Web.

Part 3: "Jeremy Scahill on Biden's 'War Against Whistleblowers,' from Daniel Ellsberg to Edward Snowden." *Democracy Now!* democracynow.org, 28 Apr. 2021. Web.

Scahill, Jeremy and Paul Abowd. *Video: Empire Politician*. *Intercept*, 27 Apr. 2021. Web.

Scahill, Jeremy and Glenn Greenwald. "The NSA's Secret Role in The U.S. Assassination Program." *Intercept*, 10 Feb. 2014. Web.

Schmitt, Eric and Helen Cooper. "Pentagon acknowledges Aug. 29 drone strike in Afghanistan was a tragic mistake that killed 10 civilians." *New York Times*, 17 Sept., updated 3 Nov. 2021. Web.

Seligman, Lara. "U.S., Iraqi officials to announce U.S. military shift to advisory role by year's end. *Politico*, 22 July 2021. Web.

Shah, Anup. "The Bush Doctrine of Pre-emptive Strikes; A Global *Pax Americana*." *Global Issues*, last updated 24 Apr. 2004. Web.

Sikorski, Radoslaw. "on Europe's role amid American and Chinese tensions." *The Economist*, 27 Aug. 2021. Web.

Sjursen, Danny. "The Empire Comes Home: Counterinsurgency,

Policing, and the Militarization of American Cities."
TomDispatch.com, 12 Oct. 2017. Web.

Sorensen, Christian. "A People's Guide to the War Industry."
Consortium News, 25 May 2021. Web.

Staff and agencies. "Bush rejects Taliban offer to hand Bin Laden
over." *The Guardian,* 14 Oct. 2001. Web.

Swain, Elise. "Joe Biden's Silence On Ending The Drone Wars:
With scant comments about U.S. assassination programs, there
are indications that Biden would keep the drone wars
around." *Intercept,* 22 Nov. 2020. Web.

Theoharis, Liz. "An American Spiritual Death Spiral?"
TomDispatch, 4 Apr. 2021. Web.

Trenin, Dmitri. "on Russia's interests in the new global order."
The Economist, 1 Oct. 2021. Web.

Turse, Nick. "The Journalist and the Fixer: Who Makes the Story
Possible?" *TomDispatch.com,* 5 Oct. 2017. Web.

Ward, Alex. "Trump has tripled the pace of US bombing in
Afghanistan." *Vox,* 21 Nov. 2017. Web.

Weil, Simone and Rachel Bespaloff. *War and the Iliad.* Tr. Mary
McCarthy. *New York Review of Books,* 2005. Print.

Whitlock, Craig and Bob Woodward. "Pentagon buries evidence
of $125 billion in bureaucratic waste." *Washington Post,* 5
Dec. 2016. Web.

Wikipedia, the free encyclopedia. Web.

Wilkie, Christina. "Biden's foreign policy team lays out a national
security vision that differs sharply from Trump's." *CNBC,* 24
Nov. 2020.

Zeese, Kevin. "As US Empire Fails, Trump Enters a Quagmire."
Counterpunch.org, 29 Aug. 2017. Web.

Acknowledgments

I am grateful to the editors of the publications in which many of the poems in this book, or earlier versions of them, have appeared:

What Part of Liberate Don't You Understand? Omega: On Line Journal of Literary Arts. Ed. Michael Annis. July 2003–September 2003: "The Swallows of Baghdad," "The Rite of Night," "Afterimage," "Immigrant Eyes," "Album I," "Album II," "Carpe Diem."

Poets Against the War, 2003: "Before War," "and the stars do not want it."

VoicesinWartime.org, 25 October 2005: "Concerto Grosso."

Ecografías Septentrional. Ed. María Merced Nájera Migoni. Delicias, Chihuahua: Chihuahua Arde Editoras, noviembre 2005: "Botas del desierto" (Tr. of "Desert Boots").

"Expresso." Correo de Guanajuato. Ed. Hilda Anchondo. 18 february 2006: "Caminan a nuestro lado" (Tr. of "They Walk among Us") and "Mamá Bonita" (Tr. of poem by the same name).

HereAfter the Coup. Omega: On Line Journal of Literary Arts. Ed. Michael Annis. July 2006: "Two Flags."

Va de Nuez: Revista Trimestral de Literatura y Artes. Ed. María del Rosario Orozco. Guadalajara, Febrero–Abril 2007: "La lavacuerpos" (Tr. of "The Bodywasher").

The Blue Guitar: The Arts and Literary Journal of the Arizona Consortium for the Arts. Ed. Rebecca Dyer. Phoenix, April 2009: "Blue Man," "The Kiss," "...but this is a birdless zone," "The Choicest Flower."

from hive this mind. Omega: On Line Journal of Literary Arts. Ed. Michael Annis. October 2009: "The Murdered," "Carding," "Not my Son!" "Pink Alert or Happy Is the Color of Subversion."

Memoria del VII Encuentro Iberoamericano de Escritores "Bajo el Asedio de los Signos." Comp. Ismael Serna. Cd. Obregón, Sonora, noviembre 2009: "Esperando a los bárbaros" (Tr. of "Waiting for the Barbarians").

"Para ti...," Suplemento Cultural. Ed. Martha Durazzo. *El Dictamen:Decano de la Prensa Nacional.* Veracruz, 18 julio 2010: "Esperando a los bárbaros" (Tr. of "Waiting for the Barbarians").

The Blue Guitar: The Arts and Literary Journal of the Arizona Consortium for the Arts. Ed. Rebecca Dyer. Phoenix, Summer 2010: "into the lizard's eyes."

Rancho Las Voces: Revista de Arte y Cultura. Ed. Rubén Moreno Valenzuela. Cd. Juárez, different issues from 2010 to 2013: "Dinastía" (Tr. of "Dynasty"), "Botas del desierto" (Tr. of "Desert Boots"), "La crucifixión puesta al día" (Tr. of "Crucifixion Update"), "Caminan a nuestro lado" (Tr. of "They Walk among Us"), "Dos banderas" (Tr. of "Two Flags"), "Excedente del ejército" (Tr. of "Army Surplus"), "Esperando a los bárbaros" (Tr. of "Waiting for the Barbarians"), "La lavacuerpos" (Tr. of "The Bodywasher"), "Ojos de inmigrante" (Tr. of "Immigrant Eyes"), "y el cielo enrojece" (Tr. of "and the sky turns red"), "Mamá bonita" (Tr. of "Mamá bonita"), "El hombre azul" (Tr. of "Blue Man"), "Mínimo," (Tr. of "Minimal"), "... y las estrellas no lo quieren" (Tr. of "and the stars do not want it"), "Olivia" (Tr. of "Olivia"), "El sepulturero" (Tr. of "The Gravedigger"), "¡No! ¡Mi hijo no!" (Tr. of "No! Not my son!"), "Rito nocturno" (Tr. of "The Rite of Night"), "Rosa Valiente" (Tr. of "Rose Valiant"), "Mañana" (Tr. of "Tomorrow"), "...hasta que deja de revolotear" (Tr. of "until it stops fluttering"), "Peines" (Tr. of "Carding"), "Marabunta" (Tr. of "Marabunta".))

The Blue Guitar: The Arts and Literary Journal of the Arizona Consortium for the Arts. Ed. Rebecca Dyer. Phoenix, Summer 2011: "Poison Letter," "The Soldier's Words."

The Blue Guitar: The Arts and Literary Journal of the Arizona Consortium for the Arts. Ed. Rebecca Dyer. Phoenix, Spring 2013: "Bulletproofing," "Let them wear mink."

Al-Mutanabbi Street Starts Here. Ed. Beau Beausoleil and Deema Shehabi. Oakland: PM Press, 2012: "into the lizard's eyes."

Sonarida: Revista de encuentro entre Sonora y Arizona. Ed. Inés Martínez de Castro. Hermosillo, enero-junio 2012: "Esperando a los bárbaros," "Waiting for the Barbarians."

About Atmosphere Press

Atmosphere Press is an independent, full-service publisher for excellent books in all genres and for all audiences. Learn more about what we do at atmospherepress.com.

We encourage you to check out some of Atmosphere's latest releases, which are available at Amazon.com and via order from your local bookstore:

Poems for the Bee Charmer (And Other Familiar Ghosts), poetry by Jordan Lentz

Flowers That Die, poetry by Gideon Halpin

Through The Soul Into Life, poetry by Shoushan B

Embrace The Passion In A Lover's Dream, poetry by Paul Turay

Reflections in the Time of Trumpius Maximus, poetry by Mark Fishbein

Drifters, poetry by Stuart Silverman

As a Patient Thinks about the Desert, poetry by Rick Anthony Furtak

Winter Solstice, poetry by Diana Howard

Blindfolds, Bruises, and Break-Ups, poetry by Jen Schneider

INHABITANT, poetry by Charles Crittenden

Godless Grace, poetry by Michael Terence O'Brien

March of the Mindless, poetry by Thomas Walrod

In the Village That Is Not Burning Down, poetry by Travis Nathan Brown

Mud Ajar, by Hiram Larew

To Let Myself Go, poetry by Kimberly Olivera Lainez

About the Author

Lilvia Soto, Ph.D., poet, essayist, and independent researcher, was a professor of Spanish American literature at Harvard University and an administrator (Assistant Dean) at the University of Pennsylvania. She was the first director of La Casa Latina: The University of Pennsylvania Center for Hispanic Excellence and the Resident Director of the Study Abroad Program in Seville, Spain, for students of Cornell, Michigan, and the University of Pennsylvania.

Soto was born in Nuevo Casas Grandes, Chihuahua, Mexico, and migrated to the United States at the age of fifteen. She resides in Philadelphia, Pennsylvania. She has published poetry, short fiction, essays, literary criticism, and literary translations in journals and anthologies in many countries. Her collection of bilingual poems, *bajo las palabras / under the words*, appeared in Editorial Garabatos, Hermosillo, Sonora, in 2015. Her second collection of bilingual poems, *Lengua lanzadera enhebrada / Tongue Threaded Shuttle,* was published in 2017, also in Editorial Garabatos. She is preparing a collection of poems and essays about her ancestors in the context of the Mexican Revolution. Lilvia is a member of the art collective We Are You Project International (**www.weareyouproject.org**). You can read some of her works at **www.lilviasoto.com.**